OSPREY AIRCRAFT OF THE [illegible]

Dolphin and Snipe [illegible]es of World War 1

SERIES EDITOR: TONY HOLMES

OSPREY AIRCRAFT OF THE ACES® • 48

Dolphin and Snipe Aces of World War 1

Norman Franks

OSPREY PUBLISHING

Front cover
At 0720 hrs on the morning of 15 August 1918, American Lt Edgar Taylor from Central Falls, Rhode Island, claimed a kite balloon shot down in flames over Estaires for his second victory – he would destroy a further three *Drachens* prior to his death in combat just nine days later. He had been transferred to No 79 Sqn at Beauvois, in France, in April 1918 but had been a slow starter. Indeed, he had failed to gain his first victory until early August. Taylor then took on the challenge of balloon busting, destroying four of these dangerous targets during the same month, but in the process of claiming his last victim near Sailly sur la Lys on the 24th, he was hit by ground fire and mortally wounded.

Edgar Taylor has no known grave, and was he was just 20 years of age when he died of his injuries, possibly in German hands, the day after claiming his fifth victim to 'make ace'.

Lt Taylor had gained all five of his successes at the controls of Dolphin D3727, which was adorned with the individual letter 'J' aft of the white squadron marking – the latter was also repeated on the top surface of the port wing, just inboard of the roundel. D3727 was on squadron strength from 16 June until it was lost on 24 August, having flown 97 hours by the time of its demise in action (*Cover artwork by Iain Wyllie*)

First published in Great Britain in 2002 by Osprey Publishing
Elms Court, Chapel Way, Botley, Oxford, OX2 9LP

ISBN 1 84176 317 9

Edited by Tony Holmes
Page design by Tony Truscott
Cover Artwork by Iain Wyllie
Aircraft Profiles by Harry Dempsey
Scale Drawings by Mark Styling
Origination by Grasmere Digital Imaging, Leeds, UK
Printed in Hong Kong through Bookbuilders

02 03 04 05 06 10 9 8 7 6 5 4 3 2 1

EDITOR'S NOTE
To make this best-selling series as authoritative as possible, the Editor would be interested in hearing from any individual who may have relevant photographs, documentation or first-hand experiences relating to the elite pilots, and their aircraft, of the various theatres of war. Any material used will be credited to its original source. Please write to Tony Holmes at 10 Prospect Road, Sevenoaks, Kent, TN13 3UA, Great Britain, or via e-mail at – tony.holmes@osprey-jets.freeserve.co.uk

CONTENTS

THE DOLPHIN

The Dolphin and Snipe were the last two fighter aircraft from the Sopwith Aviation Company stable to be produced and see action in World War 1. Both were unique in their own way, the Dolphin being designed with the unusual (and not over-liked) back-stagger of the top wing, while the Snipe would undoubtedly have re-equipped many of the Royal Air Force's Camel squadrons in the frontline had the war continued into 1919. Although it could still generally hold its own in combat, the Camel was fast becoming obsolete in fighter-versus-fighter engagements, and it had become increasingly used in the ground attack role since the late spring of 1918.

As a Camel replacement, the Dolphin was unique in that it was the first multi-gun fighter to see action during World War 1. It was also the first active Sopwith machine not to be fitted with a rotary engine. The Dolphin was designed with two belt-fed 0.303-in Vickers machine guns mounted in the by now familiar position right in front of the cockpit windscreen. Straight ahead of the pilot's line of sight, they were both fixed (through the employment of Constantinesco interrupter gear) to fire through the propeller.

The aircraft was also capable of having two drum-fed 0.303-in Lewis guns fixed to the cockpit cross-member connecting the two upper wings. The pilot could fire these upwards from a fixed position, or move either one in a similar way to guns fitted to the top wing of both the French Nieuport Scouts of 1916-17 or the British SE 5 machines. Added to this, at least one squadron experimented with two Lewis guns fitted to the uppersurfaces of the two lower wings, set to fire outside the propeller arc, although once fired, the ammunition drums could obviously not be replaced in the air.

Sopwith 5F1 Dolphin C3839 was part of the intial production batch of 500 aircraft built by the company at its Canbury Park Road factory in Kingston-upon-Thames

This pilot's eye view of the Dolphin cockpit shows the array of dials and the butts of the two Vickers machine guns. On the right of the forward cross member is a mounting bracket for a Lewis gun (*via Bruce Robertson*)

Dolphin Lineage

Even as the Sopwith Camel was beginning to roll off the production lines in the spring of 1917, Sopwith's chief designer, Herbert Smith, was working at the company's Kingston-upon-Thames factory in Surrey on an improved fighting scout. He understood that a fighter pilot needed good all-round visibility from the cockpit of his machine, and realised that the Camel, like the Pup and Triplane before it, had its fair share of 'blind spots', particularly above the upper wing.

Smith knew that improvements were needed, and he was determined that his next design would have no such obstruction from the upper wing. He therefore produced a prototype which put the pilot's eye-line above the upper wings, but still allowed him to look down to both front and rear, even though a blind-spot remained due to the lower wings. The upper wings had no centre section, being merely attached to an open rectangular frame centrally located above the cockpit, thus giving the pilot an unobstructed view above him. He could also look along the top wings to the left and right. As a result of this unique arrangement, Smith had little choice but to adopt negative back stagger of 13 inches for the upper wings in order to place the lower wings correctly.

Another view of a Dolphin cockpit. This machine has an additional elevated tubular appendage which was designed to protect the pilot should the aircraft turn over in the event of a crash-landing. Fears of this gradually subsided once the aircraft had been in frontline service for a few months, but on this particular Dolphin a Lewis gun has also been fitted to the top of the support bar

A rare view of a Dolphin in flight. This machine has extra supports fitted to each of the inner wing struts, these again being added to help protect the pilot in the event of a turn over on landing. Like the support bar fitted above the cockpit, these were later discarded

As previously mentioned, the Dolphin was the first Sopwith type to have an in-line water-cooled engine rather than the more usual air-cooled rotary, so the new fighter looked very different from other Sopwith machines, all of which had rotary engines (i.e. the propeller and engine turned together).

The aircraft's in-line engine was built around the water-cooled 200-hp geared V8 Hispano-Suiza 8B, which was now the standard fit in the newer SE 5 and French SPAD XIII fighters.

The new Sopwith type was given the Sopwith designation 5F.1, and by the spring of 1917 the first four prototype machines had been produced. The first example was passed by the Sopwith Design Department on 23 May 1917, and the following month it was flown to Martlesham Heath for its official assessment. A prototype Dolphin was subsequently flown to France on 13 June by Capt H T Tizard (later Sir Henry) to General Headquarters Royal Flying Corps (RFC) for evaluation 'In the Field' by such luminaries as Capt William 'Billy' Bishop of No 60 Sqn. On 29 June, following the successful completion of this trial, the Ministry of Munitions placed its largest order to date when it instructed Sopwith to build 500 Dolphins. Yet despite this impressive order, only four units would see operational service with the Dolphin.

Just like the Camel, Smith had designed his new machine with all the mass – engine, guns, petrol tanks and pilot – grouped together 'up front', so that the Dolphin would inherit the same high degree of manoeuvrability. The first Dolphin had a large oval air intake below the propeller which housed a radiator that cooled the water being pumped through the engine, but this gave the machine a blunt appearance that obviously impacted adversely on forward speed.

This arrangement was changed with the second prototype, two radiators being placed instead on either side of the fuselage aft of the engine cowling. This allowed the nose to take on a far sleeker, tapered and more streamlined appearance.

A brand new Dolphin is put through its paces at low level at Brooklands, in Surrey, in early 1918. Note the absence of the over wing inner struts supports

Pilots (from No 19 Sqn) who flew the fourth prototype in France in mid-1917 found that it stalled rather quickly, and that due to the peculiar shape of the nose, an inexperienced pilot had difficulty in keeping it lined up with the horizon. However, those that flew the Dolphin thought it speedier that the Camel and more manoeuvrable than the (early) SE 5. Of the dozen pilots who were able to take the fighter aloft between 15 November and 7 December, all were 'delighted' with it. A few days later, on the 12th, Capt P Huskinson took the machine up after some German Gotha bombers, in company with four of the squadron's SPAD VIIs. Although he started to catch up with the bombers, he had been forbidden from crossing the frontline, and as they neared he had, reluctantly, to break away and return to Bailleul aerodrome.

The initial pilot test reports indicated that the Dolphin could reach a speed of just under 120 knots, but as the Air Speed Indicator only went up to this indicated speed, and the needle was hard up against the notch when the fighter was in flight at ground level, a higher speed was assumed possible. On an early flight it was pitted against a Camel, and the Dolphin pilot had little problem keeping the Camel at bay, while the Camel pilot seemed powerless to get into any attacking position on the new machine.

After modifications (necessary with all new aeroplane types), the Dolphin, by the autumn of 1917, was well on the way to being produced in small numbers. Trials at Martlesham Heath and in France had shown the Dolphin to possess excellent performance and handling at high altitude – above 20,000 ft – as well as at lower heights. And although designed to carry two Lewis guns on the cockpit frame, it was being recommended by test pilots with operational experience on other fighter types that it should only have one, plus of course the two regular cockpit-mounted Vickers guns.

Seven-victory ace Capt E D Crundall DFC, who had flown Sopwith Triplanes and Camels with 8 Naval Air Squadron and No 210 Sqn RAF, shared his fond memories of the Dolphin with me in a letter he once wrote to me about the Sopwith fighter;

Stripped of its linen by souvenir hunters, Dolphin C3791 'R' of No 79 Sqn presents a sorry sight behind enemy lines. While not an ace's aircraft, it was shot down by an ace, Leutnant Rudolf Stark of *Jasta* 34b, on 30 March 1918. Its pilot, 2Lt H W Browne, was taken prisoner (*via Jon Guttman*)

Future SE 5 aces Larry Callahan (of the USAS) and M C McGregor, with Lt Abbott far right, take a break at Hounslow during their training on the Dolphin in early 1918. These men were all assigned to No 85 Sqn, which was initially slated to receive Dolphins before being switched to SE 5s prior to heading for France in May 1918

'The Dolphin was a nice machine to fly with no vices. I did all kinds of aerobatics on this type. It was not as sensitive on the controls as the Camel and Triplane, or Pup, because it was a slightly bigger and heavier aircraft. The wings had a backwards stagger so the view upwards was very good.'

In the last weeks of 1917 the first production machines were on the verge of being sent to France to allow No 19 Sqn, flying SPAD VIIs, to re-equip with the new type. As with Capt Crundall, the battle-seasoned pilots of this unit had immediately warmed to the Dolphin during their brief evaluation of the type in the autumn, and now they looked forward to its arrival.

In Squadron Service

No 19 Sqn moved to St Marie Capel in order to begin re-equipping with the new Sopwith fighter in late December, three Dolphins arriving on the 28th and another on the 29th – the task was completed by 9 January 1918, and the pilots flew their first frontline patrols in the new fighter on 3 February. Meanwhile, No 79 Sqn, working-up at Beaulieu, in Hampshire, had also been supplied with Dolphins during December, and on 20 February it moved to France (initially St Omer, and then on to Estrée-Blanche 48 hours later) to prepare for operations.

The third squadron to equip with the Dolphin was another new unit working-up in England, No 87. Nos 87 and 85 Sqns might both have been equipped with SE 5s, but at the last moment, the former was given Dolphins, and although No 85 Sqn also flew some, it was finally decided to keep the latter exclusively equipped with the SE 5.

In France, the other SPAD-equipped RFC unit (flying SPAD XIIIs, not VIIs), No 23 Sqn, was pulled out of the line to equip with the new Dolphins, but then came the German March Offensive which commenced on the 21st. Replacement Dolphins were urgently needed by Nos 19 and 79 Sqns due to damage and losses they had suffered during the seemingly ceaseless ground attack sorties that they had flown in an

These No 87 Sqn Dolphins were photographed at Hounslow in early 1918. No unit markings have yet been applied to any of the factory-fresh fighters. Dolphin 'C' is C4159, which Capt A W Vigers MC DFC subsequently used to claim 15 victories

effort to help stem the massive German advance, and No 23 Sqn lost its aircraft to both units. Meanwhile, Hounslow-based No 87 Sqn was on the verge of being declared ready to do battle in France, but instead of tackling the Hun, the unit was ordered to hand over its Dolphins to the now depleted No 23 Sqn! However, as the danger of the March Offensive ended, No 87 Sqn was permitted to keep its machines, and the unit flew across the Channel on 25 April to St Omer, before moving on to Petite Synthe – one of the Dunkirk aerodromes – three days later.

INTO COMBAT

No 19 Sqn had been in action in France since August 1916, initially flying BE 12s and, from October 1916, SPAD VIIs. It had seen a good deal of combat during 1917, and many of its pilots had become aces, including Maj A D Carter, Capts J Leacroft, F Sowrey, O C Bryson and P Huskinson, and Lts A A N D Pentland and E Olivier. Some of these famous names had left the squadron by the time the first Dolphins arrived, but others switched to the new type quite easily and continued to score victories.

Combat ready on the new machine by mid February 1918, No 19 Sqn moved back to Bailleul on the 13th of that month and began operations. The unit was still commanded by Maj W D S Sanday DSO MC at this time, the major having led the unit since the previous April. He was replaced the following month by Maj E R Pretyman, who remained in command until war's end.

The unit did not get off to a good start with the new fighter, its first few patrols being attacked by British aircraft whose pilots were unfamiliar

A bevy of No 19 Sqn aces who flew both SPADs and Dolphins are seen in this group photograph, taken in March 1918. They are, seated from left to right, Maj A D Carter DSO (29 victories), Maj W D S Sanday MC (squadron CO – five victories) and Capt P Huskinson MC (11 victories). Standing behind, again from left to right, are Lts A B Fairclough (19 victories), J D I Hardman (nine victories), H V Puckridge (one victory) and E Olivier (eight victories), Capt J Leacroft (22 victories) and Lts G B Irving (12 victories) and Lord (partially cropped off the original print). Between them, these nine fighter pilots (Lord was the squadron adjutant) were credited with 116 victories in World War 1

Maj Sanday (standing in the cockpit) poses with one of No 19 Sqn'a first Dolphins – C3828 'P'. Leutnant Paul Billik of *Jasta* 52 downed this machine on 3 May 1918 whilst it was being flown by Capt G Chadwick, who became a Prisoner of War (PoW) (*Bruce/Leslie collection*)

with the type and assumed they must be German. Fortunately, none of the Dolphin pilots were shot down. The comment was made, however, that the Sopwith fighter looked decidedly 'Hunnish', and Dolphin pilots took extra care in subsequent weeks whenever friendly aircraft appeared to be taking an interest in them.

It may be of interest to know something of the problems No 19 Sqn had with its first Dolphins. One supposes that all new types have teething troubles, but it is amazing sometimes to learn how many changes and alterations have to be made at operational squadron level, which really should have been ironed out if not at the factory, at least at the aircraft acceptance parks. On 2 January 1918, Maj W D S Sanday had had to report problems with two Dolphins which the squadron were testing. Both machines shed their propellers, complete with bosses, keys and lock nuts as they were run-up from cold, doing about 500 and 800 rpm respectively. The bosses on the trailing end of the key-way also burst. The three leading threads on one gear shaft were also stripped.

On 22 February 1918, Maj Sanday made out the following report to No 11 Wing Headquarters (which also appear to double as some form of pilot's notes), recording that there was little difference in flying Dolphins from other machines, and the best speed for climbing was thought to be 75 mph. Based on his pilots' experiences he continued;

'When diving, it has been found that engines pick up better if the compensator is left open, and then adjusted when the throttle is opened again.

'Both petrol tanks should never be used at the same time, and when one tank is finished, the petrol cap and the pressure tap for that tank should be turned off at once. When starting, the bottom petrol tank tap and the corresponding pressure tap should be turned on and the pressure pumped up, but never pump pressure into both tanks at the same time, and never have both petrol taps turned on at the same time. Tanks should never be filled too full.

'To use the top tank as gravity, turn off bottom tank and bottom pressure, turn on top petrol and pressure and open the release valve. Pressure valve at bottom of hand pump is more or less useless in its present position, and a tap should be fitted in the petrol pipe in a convenient position.

'The oil gauge should have a tap, which should be turned off until the engine has been running for some minutes, otherwise the gauges become unserviceable owing to pressure being considerably above their register while the oil is cold.

'Running of engine – the most extreme care should be exercised in the running of the engine in cold weather where the oil is thick. It should be run for ten minutes very slowly, otherwise the strain on the pump spindle will be so excessive that there is a grave risk of rupture.

'The squadron makes the following alterations to Dolphins which are arriving at present;

'1. Reinforce oil tank, which is very weak, especially where the neck joins the tank.

'2. Put a slide under machine to enable mechanics to get oil reservoir, etc.

'3. Cut and lace fuselage.

'4. Put doors on ammunition boxes.

'5. Add release valve for pressure system.

'6. Put a special locking devise on the propeller boss.

'7. Grind boss of propeller on to shaft very carefully – when fixing propeller to boss, put powdered resin on both faces of propeller.

'8. Fit ring sight – special ring sight has been made.

'9. Taps have been fitted to tops of radiators.'

A Edgar Peatfield was a mechanic with No 19 Sqn during this period, and I have a letter from him regarding Maj Sanday's standing orders for the new machine;

'I have an order of the day issued by the CO which gives various advice to all pilots in regard to the operation of the taps for controlling the main and reserve petrol tanks – also on the best throttle settings for climbing speeds, etc. On several occasions it was discovered that some crashes were caused by pilots siphoning petrol from one tank to another, thus starving the engine. This was due to the inability of some pilots not understanding the principle of operation. I remember a very well known flight commander crashing shortly after returning from leave – he had apparently forgotten how to operate the taps.'

Although of indifferent quality, this photograph is worthy of inclusion by dint of the fact that three of these Dolphins were flown by No 19 Sqn aces – 'A' was used by Roger Del'Haye (nine victories), 'B' by John DePencier (eight victories) and 'D' by Norm Hustings (seven victories). The final machine, 'C', was assigned to Lt W A Hunter (*via R Lowry*)

One of the first recorded combats had taken place six days prior to this report when, on 16 February 1918, Maj A D Carter engaged a number of two-seater reconnaissance machines, although a broken gunsight hampered success. The next day, he and two companions engaged another enemy machine, but this time his engine failed as he closed in, and the second Dolphin had an inner bay front flying wire snap. By this time the German was well on his way home. On the same patrol, Oliver Bryson went after a two-seater, only to have oil gush back from the engine and blind him.

On the 21st Pat Huskinson joined five Bristol F 2B Fighters attacking a German machine, but his guns refused to fire and he had to sit helplessly as the 'Brisfits' brought down their adversary.

These were not auspicious beginnings for the Dolphin, but on the 26th, during a mid-morning low patrol of the frontline, Lts J DePencier, C V Gardner and J L McLintock engaged a pair of German two-seaters. However, they were in turn attacked by three German fighters, led by a Fokker Dr I, which latched onto McLintock's tail. John DePencier was able to fire at the triplane and force it down in a spin, but McLintock was last seen gliding towards the ground south-west of Comines, and he was later reported as being prisoner.

He had been flying B6871, which had been the fourth prototype machine, and had been issued to No 19 Sqn on 15 November 1917. The Dr I pilot, Leutnant Richard Plange of *Jasta* 2 (Boelcke), survived the attack by DePencier and returned home to claim his third victory of an eventual seven kills. In fact he claimed a SPAD, showing that the Germans were not aware of the new British type at the front, and presumably Plange discounted it being a Camel or SE 5 and was left with a SPAD, as the French scout also had two sets of wing struts like the Dolphin. He might have claimed a Bristol Fighter, as others were to do, for these two sets of wing struts gave the appearance of it being an F 2B as well.

Manfred von Richthofen was to fall into this trap on 27 March when he claimed a Bristol Fighter instead of a Dolphin of No 79 Sqn for his 73rd victory. By this time No 79 Sqn had been in France for almost a week, based at Estrée-Blanche, under the command of Maj Maurice Waldegrave Noel.

The son of an army colonel, Noel came from Gloucester and had been in France since the start of the war with No 15 Sqn. His three flight commanders were experienced airmen as well. Capt W M Fry MC was

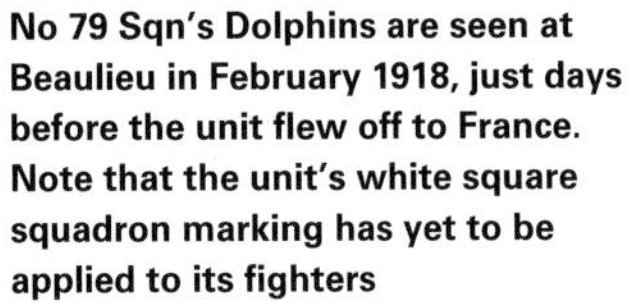

No 79 Sqn's Dolphins are seen at Beaulieu in February 1918, just days before the unit flew off to France. Note that the unit's white square squadron marking has yet to be applied to its fighters

already an ace on Nieuports with No 60 Sqn and SPADs with No 23 Sqn. Capts H P Rushforth MC and F S Williams commanded the other two flights. Most of the squadrons remaining pilots were new to France, however. Henry Philip Rushforth, from Ealing, West London, had flown with No 27 Sqn in early 1917, before becoming a flight commander with No 85 Sqn when it was forming. He then moved to No 79 Sqn. Rushforth was wounded on 20 May 1918, and upon returning to the unit, was wounded again on 7 September.

The first confirmed destruction of a German aircraft by a Dolphin came on 8 March. During a morning Offensive Patrol (OP), four red-tailed Albatros scouts were engaged by No 19 Sqn. Capt Bryson fired at one and the German's wings came off, and Capt Huskinson attacked another, which went down 'out of control'.

It is never easy to say for certain 'who got who' in these combats, but Bryson's claim, which was his first and only Dolphin victory (and brought his score to 12), was over Gheluvelt at 1110 hrs, in C3837.

These pilots were photographed at Hounslow during No 87 Sqn's training period with the Dolphin in 1918. They are, from left to right, Capt H J Larkin, Lt J W Warner (of No 85 Sqn, which was also transitioning onto the Sopwith fighter at the same time), Lt H A R Biziou and Lt T T Shipman. The first three men would become aces, and Shipman a PoW

Offizierstellvertreter Willi Kampe of *Jasta* 27 was killed in this location at 1208 German time (which at this period was one hour ahead of Allied time), although he is thought to have been lost in combat with DH 4 bombers of No 27 Sqn. But this unit was operating much further south, so Bryson's victim may well have been eight-victory ace Kampe, or a *Jasta* 51 pilot who went down near Rumbeke, south of the Gheluvelt location, and losing the wings of his aircraft in the process.

Dolphin D5315 'K' No 23 Sqn was photographed at the unit's Advanced Landing Ground (ALG) at Faucaucourt in September 1918 (*Bruce/Leslie collection*)

Capt W M Fry MC had seen action flying SPAD VIIs and XIIIs with Nos 60 and 23 Sqns prior to joining No 79 Sqn as a flight commander in early 1918. He claimed his 11th, and final, victory on 11 May 1918, flying Dolphin C4180. In this particular photograph Fry is seen posing with a No 23 Sqn SPAD XIII in December 1917. He was OC 'C Flight' at the time

No 87 Sqn was by now working up in England and preparing to fly to France. Commanded by another experienced pilot, Maj J C Callaghan MC, its flight commanders were former No 19 Sqn ace Capt A A N D Pentland MC, Capt C J W Darwin, who had flown Martinsydes with No 27 Sqn, and Capt H J Larkin CdG, formally a two-seat RE 8 pilot. Again, most of the remaining pilots were new to air combat, although at least three had been observers in France prior to pilot training, and one was an ex-SPAD pilot.

No 23 Sqn had been ear-marked to be the fourth Dolphin unit, and in March it moved from Bertangles to St Omer to re-equip. It was commanded by Maj C E Bryant DSO, and having been in action with SPAD VIIs (and subsequently XIIIs) since the beginning of 1917, its pilots were mostly experienced air fighters.

Capt W M Fry MC was one of its flight commanders, and he had 'made ace' flying Nieuports with No 60 Sqn prior to joining No 23 Sqn, and before going on to No 79 Sqn as previously mentioned in this chapter. Capt H F S Drewitt MC was another SPAD ace, while Capt J Fitz-Morris MC (sometimes referred to as J F Morris) was the third flight commander. He had achieved ace status on both DH 4 bombers and SPAD scouts.

THE GERMAN MARCH OFFENSIVE

The German army commenced its massive Operation *Michael* on 21 March 1918. Faced with the imminent influx of American troops into the war, and with the end of the war on the Russian front having released large numbers of German soldiers, the German High Command knew it was now or never in France. While not totally unexpected, the might of the attack along the British front overwhelmed the defenders and pushed them rapidly back – the greatest in-road into the Allied line since early in the war.

The RFC was soon hard-pressed to combat the German air armada which supported its troops on the ground. It was also called on to flying almost non-stop ground attack sorties in a valiant attempt to stem the tide of field-grey uniformed troops that seemed unstoppable. Camels, SE 5s, Bristols, DH 4s and 'Big Acks' all flew low level bombing and strafing attacks, while the Corps machines – mostly RE 8s – endeavoured to locate the advancing soldiers and direct shell-fire onto them.

This Dolphin has had its starboard Vickers gun and the top section of its engine cowling removed so as to allow maintenance to be performed on its Hispano-Suiza engine. The aircraft's pilot, Lt Golding, surveys the exposed engine from his cockpit

The Dolphins of Nos 19 and 79 Sqns were quickly pressed into service, and the latter unit suffered a number of losses to ground fire. No 19 Sqn also had numerous aircraft damaged, but only actually lost three Dolphins during this period. No 79 Sqn, however, needed replacement aircraft as well as flight commanders, having lost two of the latter. The result was that No 23 Sqn had to pass its recently acquired aircraft onto No 79 Sqn as attrition replacements, and in turn wait for No 87 Sqn to fly over to France from Hounslow with its Dolphins, which were now officially assigned to No 23 Sqn! The latter unit also sent Capts Fry and Drewitt to replace lost the flight commanders in No 79 Sqn.

As the offensive gradually petered out in early April, the Dolphin pilots were able to resume their activities in the upper air, seeking out German aircraft to combat.

APRÈS LA GUERRE

Once the war ended, three of the four Dolphin units were almost immediately reduced to cadre or

This official Sopwith factory photograph of a fully armed Dolphin was taken on 15 February 1918. This machine lacks an Aldis gun sight, which would normal protrude through the hole in the windscreen. The rectangular-shaped apparatus just forward of the fuselage roundel is the starboard flank radiator – an identical piece of equipment was fitted in exactly the same place on the port side of the fuselage . . .

. . . as this rear view of the same machine clearly shows. Note how the exhaust stubs flare out and away from the fuselage sides

soon disbanded. The only one to survive for any length of time was No 79 Sqn, which formed part of the Army of Occupation, based at Bickersdorf. Pilots who were not demobbed immediately – especially those from Nos 23, 79 and 87 Sqns, formed the nucleus of No 79 Sqn in Germany, but in July 1919 it too was disbanded.

AMERICAN INTEREST

In mid 1918 the Americans took an interest in the Dolphin, probably at a time when the Nieuport 28s were being phased out and replaced with SPAD XIIIs. Considering the number of Dolphins ordered, there was no doubt an excess in England looking for good homes.

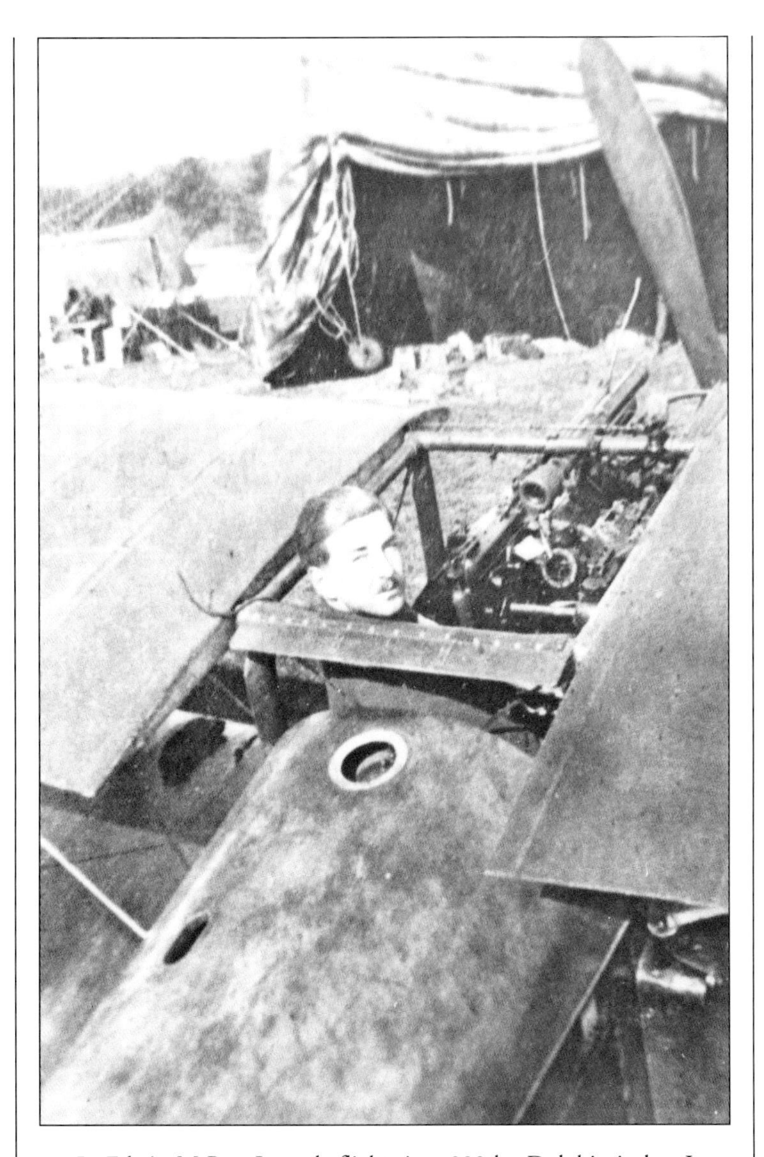

No 87 Sqn five-kill Dolphin ace Lt C E Worthington relaxes in the cockpit of his fighter in France in 1918. This view clearly shows just how good the vision was for a Dolphin pilot. Note the Aldis gun sight, and the 'C Flight' wheel (painted all white) propped up inside the makeshift canvas hangar. Immediately behind the cockpit is the filler cap for the fighter's seven-gallon gravity tank

1Lt Edwin M Post Jr made flights in a 300 hp Dolphin in late June 1918. He found it steady in flight, which he thought would facilitate accurate shooting. It was not nose-heavy and answered all controls readily. Landing was extremely easy at about 50 mph. When Post considered the manoeuvrability of the Dolphin, he found it extraordinary for a machine carrying such a load (1047 kg on take off), and at height, handled better than the SPAD. It gave the pilot ideal vision, and he could make a 180-degree turn in eight seconds.

While 1Lt Post seemed very pleased with the Dolphin, it was not chosen by the United States Air

The third airframe of the third batch of (200) Dolphins ordered, Sopwith-built D3578 'B' of No 79 Sqn survived the final months of the war to see service with the Army of Occupation in Germany. The unit was based at Bickendorf, near Köln, until it was disbanded on 15 July 1919 (*via L A Rogers*)

Service, who undoubtedly favoured the SPAD, as much for political reasons as any other. And there was no shortage of them. SPAD XIIIs duly became the main, and only mount, of American pursuit squadrons in France from the late summer onwards, with the exception of the two Camel-equipped units which flew with the British.

More No 79 Sqn Dolphins are seen at Bickendorf post-war. 'N' (C8189) was used by Capt F J Stevenson to claim three victories in the last week of the war, while 'Q' (E4756) was the mount of 17-kill ace Capt Ronald Bannerman in 1919. Finally, 'M' (E4728) was flown by Lt H Parsons in Germany

SPECIAL FEATURES

The Sopwith Dolphin, apart from being able to use between three and six guns, had other qualities which set it apart from the Camel and SE 5 – it should be emphasised, however, that it was rare for a Dolphin pilot to carry six guns. Despite authority frowning on the use of two Lewis guns in addition to the twin Vickers guns, a number of pilots did carry and use the two Lewis, but more often than not just carried one. It was a useful addition to have if it became necessary to fire upwards in a tight situation,

No 87 Sqn's Maj J C Callaghan chose Dolphin C4168 as his assigned machine when he took command of the unit in February 1918. The aircraft is seen at Hounslow soon after Callaghan had replaced Capt C J W Darwin as CO

Although not an ace, Canadian Capt Frederick J Stevenson was awarded a DFC for this three-kill haul in the final week of World War 1. He is standing in the Bickendorf mud in front of 'his' 'N' (C8189) in early 1919

but many pilots eventually decided against the single or double Lewis arrangement and just used the two fixed Vickers guns.

The advantage of being able to have a good all-round view, especially above, was not lost on the Dolphin pilots, although to many it felt strange at first to have one's head above the wings. There was thought to be an inherent danger of suffering a broken neck in a rough or forced landing were the aeroplane to turn over onto its back, and in the early days a couple of cabane half hoops were fitted to the top wing either side of the cockpit area to support the structure in the event of a turn-over. However, there is possibly only one recorded severe injury to a pilot whose machine did turn-turtle in a frontline unit, so these hoops (or crash bars) too were soon discarded, although they were often retained in Dolphin training schools.

Pilots found the Dolphin very manoeuvrable, and as the early test pilots had discovered, the aircraft enjoyed the luxury of being able to fly at high altitudes without much loss of performance. In fact, in the Dolphin's early days, at a time when German two-seater photo-reconnaissance aircraft still operated over the Allied lines, it was the high-flying Dolphins which combated these intrusions, shooting down a number of Rumplers and driving others back over to their side of the lines.

Pilots in No 87 Sqn, mindful of the thin air above 20,000 ft, experimented with the use of an oxygen supply tank for themselves. However, when a tank was fixed just behind the seat of a wrecked Dolphin and a few Lewis rounds fired into it, the resultant explosion quickly ended that idea! As Dolphin pilot Sir Leslie Hollinghurst once told me, 'We had enough problems without worrying about having our heads blown off by some Hun hitting our oxygen tank'.

DOLPHIN ACES

No 19 Sqn

The first Dolphin ace was Capt John Leacroft MC. No youngster at 29 years old in 1918 (he had been born on 4 November 1888), Leacroft had initially served as an RFC observer in Egypt with No 14 Sqn early in the war. After pilot training, he joined No 19 Sqn in the spring of 1917, and by the end of the year had scored 14 victories. Leacroft had accounted for his all-important fifth victory when he downed two Albatros Scouts in two separate evening engagements on 1 September.

His first Dolphin successes came on 15 March 1918, by which time he was a flight commander. Leacroft claimed two Albatros D V scouts out of control, followed two days later by a Pfalz D III shot down in flames. The latter victory came during a fight which saw three Pfalz and two Albatros scouts claimed by No 19 Sqn shortly after noon in the Roulers/Menin areas. *Jasta* 28 had a pilot killed at this time and location.

Capt John Leacroft MC and Bar claimed 22 victories with No 19 Sqn, eight of which he scored with the Sopwith Dolphin

On the 23rd Leacroft and another pilot flamed a two-seater, and the next day he claimed two Albatros D Vs. In April he brought his overall score to 21, adding one more victory in May, which took his Dolphin tally to eight – the last six whilst flying Dolphin C3829.

In 1967 I asked John Leacroft for his recollections of flying the Sopwith Dolphin, to which he replied, 'I found it a very good fighting machine, and a great improvement in climb, performance and armament on the SPAD, but with less climb and "zoom" than the SE 5, which I think at that time was so essential for fighting purposes.

'To the best of my memory I cannot remember the Hispano engine being unreliable, and have no personal recollection of having had any forced landings on account of engine failure – this was probably due to the good work of the squadron mechanics.

'Towards the end of my service with No 19 Sqn we carried out patrols which, for the most part, I led with my flight. We were followed at different altitudes, but

Canadian Maj A D Carter DSO and Bar claimed 15 victories flying the SPAD, and then added a further 14 with the Dolphin. His tally of 29 kills made him No 19 Sqn's 'ace of aces'. He was shot down by *Jasta* 52 ace Leutnant Paul Billik on 19 May 1918, Carter spending the rest of the war as a PoW

in close touch, by the other two flights ("A" and "B"). These squadron-strength patrols took the place of flight patrols because of the larger packs of Huns we had to deal with, and our tactic has proven successful.'

Having won the Military Cross (MC) and Bar with No 19 Sqn, and been the unit's second highest scorer during the war, it was little wonder that Maj Leacroft remained in the RAF post-war, and by the mid-1930s he had risen to the rank of wing commander, and was then made a group captain in 1937. He subsequently retired later that year, but served again during World War 2. Retiring to the south coast of England, John Leacroft died in Bexhill-on-Sea in 1971.

The top scoring pilot in No 19 Sqn was Canadian Maj Albert Desbrisay Carter. Born on 2 June 1892 in Pointe de Bute, New Brunswick, he was a professional soldier, having joined the army in early 1911 at the age of 18. Sent to England with the Canadian Expeditionary Force (New Brunswick Regiment) and serving in the trenches on the Western Front, Carter had been promoted to major rank by February 1916, having been severely wounded in October of the previous year.

Transferring to the RFC, he became a pilot in September 1917, retaining his previous army rank. In the summer of 1917 Carter flew coastal patrols, but in the autumn he returned to France to fly SPAD VIIs with No 19 Sqn. His first victories came on the last day of October, when he claimed a C-type observation aeroplane in the morning and an Albatros D V scout in the afternoon. Carter 'made ace' with a shared victory over another Albatros D V on the afternoon of 13 November. During this month alone he added six more kills to his score, and in December, a further seven, bringing his total to 15.

These successes resulted in Carter being awarded the Distinguished ervice Order (DSO) in the New Year, together with the Belgian Croix de Guerre (CdG). He transitioned onto the Dolphin with little fuss, and continued to score in the same ruthless manner as he had done with the SPAD. Indeed, by mid-May 1918 Carter's total had reached 28, his tally including one of the first Fokker D VII fighters encountered by the Allies on the Western Front.

A typical day's action for Maj Carter in early 1918 is revealed in his combat report for 15 March. He engaged the enemy for the first time at 1115 hrs, and then took part in a second action 15 minutes later. Both encounters occurred south of Halluin;

'I dived on several EA (enemy aircraft) Scouts at 1110 am. After engaging several EA, I finally got on to one helpless EA and fired several bursts at very close range. EA started to glide down when I got on to his tail again, and simply got a straight shot. EA went down into a slow spin and disappeared from view far below, out of control.

'I dived on an EA scout which was flying above several other Scouts. I fired several bursts at very close range, alternating bursts with my Vickers and Lewis guns. The EA appeared out of control, and finally upon firing another burst at EA when stalling, the right-hand wings of the EA folded back and the EA went down in a very steep spin. I did not see EA crash, as I did not follow it down, but it was undoubtedly destroyed.'

Having studied many World War 1 combat reports, one tends to feel that the more successful aces quickly learnt how to write them – the cynical might say in a style to impress the Recording Officer whose job it was to forward such reports to 'higher authority' in order for the pilot, and unit, to be credited with a victory. Phrases such as 'very close range' and 'got a straight shot' would indicate to the reader of such a report that the pilot was closing right up with the enemy, and not just blazing away in the hope of scoring some hits.

Of these two Pfalz D III scouts claimed, certainly the one which lost both wings on one side looks a certain kill, although it has to be said that there is no obvious German casualty that fits this date. Perhaps the pilot survived a spectacular crash!

These further Dolphin victories brought Carter an unprecedented Bar to his DSO, but he was then shot down himself, on 19 May, and taken prisoner. His adversary was Leutnant Paul Billik of *Jasta* 52, the Dolphin ace being the German's 17th of an eventual 31 kills. After the war Carter returned to England, but he was killed in a flying accident on 22 May 1919 and buried in Old Shoreham Cemetery, in Sussex, aged 25. Tragically, he was flying a captured Fokker which broke up in mid-air.

Ten of Carters' 29 claims were made whilst flying Dolphin C4017.

Arthur Bradfield Fairclough was another o No 19 Sqn's successful Canadian Dolphin pilots. Born on 25 July 1896 in Toronto, his pre-war occupation was as a clerk with Messrs Wood, Gundy and Co, in the city of his birth. Having joined the Queen's Own Rifles Militia when this was mobilised as the 166th Overseas Battalion Canadian Expeditionary Force (CEF) in 1916, Fairclough sailed for England in October of that year.

He saw duty in France in 1917 as a lieutnant with the Canadian Machine Gun Corps, but then transferred to the RFC in May 1917 and, after training, found himself flying SPAD VIIs in November. Fairclough's scoring rate was exceptional, and he claimed no fewer than nine kills in December – a double in two fights on the 19th, made him an ace.

Following the arrival of the Dolphin, he had shot down five Germans by early May 1918, and was then sent to No 23 Sqn as a flight commander. By early July Fairclough had added five more kills to his score, downing a Rumpler on the 5th of that month to bring his score to 19. He received the MC (gazetted in May 1918), and with his tour at an end he returned to England in July, then home to Canada. Arthur Fairclough died on 9 December 1968 – almost 51 years to the day after he had downed his first German aeroplane.

Fellow Canadian Gordon Budd Irving, also from Toronto (born on 15 May 1898), joined the RFC in Canada during 1917 when aged 19. Once trained, he joined No 19 Sqn that November, and his first victory came on 24 March 1918. Between April and mid-June, Irving added a further seven kills flying Dolphin C3799, and by 2 July his score had risen to eleven. His luck finally ran out on 11 August, however.

By now a flight commander with the DFC, Irving had led a patrol over the battle front in the late afternoon and had got into a scrap with German fighters. Although he was seen to send a Pfalz scout down out of control, his own aircraft – E4432 – was hit, and fell burning to the ground. Two of Irving's pilots were also brought down, one being killed and the other taken prisoner, during a hectic dogfight between them and *Jastas* 10 and 23b near Albert. Leutnants Alois Heldman and Justus Grassmann each claimed Dolphins for their tenth and fifth victories respectively. Just 21 years of age when he died, Gordon Irving has no known grave.

Capt G B Irving DFC of No 19 Sqn was also a Canadian, hailing from Toronto. He scored 12 Dolphin victories before crashing to his death near Albert following a dogfight on 11 August 1918 (*via S K Taylor*)

One of No 19 Sqn's aces who would survive the war and eventually gain high rank in the RAF was even younger than Canadian Irving – James Donald Innes Hardman, a Yorkshire lad from Delph, was born on 21 December 1899. On leaving school he joined the Artist's Rifles, and then the RFC in early 1917. Commissioned, Hardman was too young to go to France until February 1918, at which time he was sent to No 19 Sqn just as it was converting to Dolphins. Despite his extreme youth, Hardman claimed nine German aircraft shot down before the war ended, earning him a Distinguished Flying Cross (DFC) and promotion to captain.

His first five kills were claimed in Dolphin C3818, which he used to great effect in a huge dogfight that took place on 30 October. Leading 12 Dolphins that were flying as escorts for DH 4s of No 98 Sqn, Hardman and his squadronmates ran into the *Jastas* of *Jagdesgeschwader* Nr.III (JG III). Five Dolphins were shot down, with one pilot killed and four taken prisoner – a sixth returned to base wounded. Four of the bombers were also shot down, with another force-landed and shelled. Two others got home with wounded crewmen on board. Hardman emerged from the clash with claims for two Fokker D VIIs destroyed, as recorded by his combat report;

'Led a patrol as escort to No 98 Sqn to Mons. Over this area at 14,000 ft at 1120 am, 14 Fokker biplanes attacked the DH 9s, and another ten attacked three of us comprising the bottom flight. Sandwiched between three formations, a running fight ensued all the way to the lines. As the EAs on the tails of the DH 9s were paying no attention to the three of us, we got in some very good shooting at them. At 1130 am I dived on one and fired a long burst into him, and he immediately burst into flames. Two miles before we got to the lines I engaged another, and after fighting him for a while, he spun down, and just before he hit the ground he also burst into flames and crashed. Most of the Fokkers left soon after this, and we turned and drove the rest away. Our last scrap took place at about 3000 ft.'

Note that Hardman has mixed the gender of opposing aeroplanes and pilots in his report, calling the aeroplane a 'he' or a 'him'. He is not alone in adopting this literary style, as the authors of a considerable number of the reports that I have studied (from both world wars) over the years have employed mixed genders. It also never ceases to amaze me how pilots always seem to know the time of these actions when one would have thought that the last thing they would have remembered to do in the heat of battle was to look at the clock!

After the war James Hardman completed his education at Oxford and returned to the RAF in 1921. Following service in World War 2, he commanded the Royal Australian Air Force on exchange from the RAF. Hardman retired in 1958 as an Air Chief Marshal GBE KCB DFC, and died on 2 March 1982. On 30 October 1968 – on the 50th anniversary of that last big dogfight – he mentioned to me;

'We were the first squadron to get Dolphins, and we kept them till the end of the war. They were excellent high up, with their two bays and plenty of lift, but the 200-hp geared Hispano was pretty unreliable. But that last fight was quite a party.'

Yet another Canadian ace in No 19 Sqn John Dartnell DePencier, who hailed from Manse, Vancouver – his 20th birthday would fall the day

Yet another Canadian ace to fly with No 19 Sqn, Capt John DePencier, claimed two SPAD and six Dolphin victories. He was killed in a flying accident over Germany in May 1920 (*via S K Taylor*)

after the Armistice. The son of the Bishop of New Westminster, he first served with the 68th Canadian Field Battery, and when he joined No 19 Sqn, in October 1917, he was still only 19. Before the month was out, DePencier had claimed his first kill in a SPAD – he had gained a second victory before the end of the year.

Once flying Dolphins in 1918, he had increased his score to eight by mid-July. On one occasion, DePencier landed his Dolphin after a dogfight believing he'd been hit in the stomach by a spent bullet, and his comrades and the squadron doctor concurred with him. Feeling a bit groggy, he had laid on his bed for a while, and when he arose he found the mattress covered in blood. A more thorough examination revealed that he had indeed been hit by a bullet, but one, far from being spent, which had actually gone right through him and out the other side without causing serious injury or hitting anything vital!

Promoted to captain, DePencier was rested in the late summer of 1918, and the following year he joined No 1 Sqn, Royal Canadian Air Force (RCAF), in England. Later, he served with No 12 Sqn, which was part of the Occupation Forces in Germany, but was killed in a mid-air collision near Cologne on 20 May 1920. The second aircraft involved was also flown by a World War 1 ace, Capt C B Ridley DSC (Triplanes and Camels). He too was killed.

The son of a farmer, Capt Cecil Vernon Gardner came from Gawcott, in Buckinghamshire, although he was actually born at Broughton in 1891 (official records also have his year of birth as being 1889). Gardner joined the RFC in March 1917 from the army, into which he had enlisted in December 1915. In between these two dates, he appears to have transferred to the RFC earlier as a 2nd Class Air Mechanic. Commissioned in July 1917, he was trained and posted to No 19 Sqn in January 1918, his age then being given as 29, so the 1889 date appears more correct!

Although he did not score his first victory until 6 June, by the end of July Gardner had become an ace, and in the action on 11 August (in which Gordon Irving was killed), he shot down a Pfalz scout from which Unteroffizier Max Bauer of *Jasta* 23b bailed out and descended safely in his parachute, although wounded. On 27 September he brought his score to ten, but was himself brought down in this action (in E4501), crashing near Bapaume. He died three days later. Gardner had been the third victim of Unteroffizier Gustav Borm of *Jasta* 1, the German going on to achieve five victories by war's end. Cecil Gardner's DFC was gazetted on 2 November 1918.

French by birth, Roger Amedee Del'Haye was born in Chalons-sur-Marne on 9 January 1889 and educated at the University of Paris. Emigrating to Canada, he settled in Regina and became a British subject in 1914. Once war became a reality, Del'Haye joined the RFC in October 1915, and served with No 13 Sqn, flying BE 2s and RE 8s, between April 1916 and May 1917. Converting to single-seaters, he went to No 19 Sqn in May 1918, and during the summer and early autumn accounted for nine German aircraft – a Fokker Dr I and eight Pfalz scouts. Del'Haye received the DFC and Belgian CdG, ending the conflict as a flight commander.

Returning to Canada after the war, Del'Haye was employed as an income tax assessor for most of the 1920s before managing an airport in

Regina until 1939. He also joined the RCAF Reserve in the 1930s, commanding No 120 Sqn RCAF. Del'Haye, who had become an air commodore by 1944, was killed on 18 November that year during a take-off crash while flying solo in a Harvard trainer.

Finley McQuiston was a veteran flyer long before he joined No 19 Sqn. A former Royal Field Artillery man, his first war flying was with No 12 Sqn in mid-1916, but he was badly wounded in September. Upon recovery, McQuiston joined No 55 Sqn, which was equipped with DH 4s, but he was wounded again in May 1917. By then he had achieved a combat victory over an Albatros scout. Fit again in 1918, and having converted to fighters, McQuiston went to No 19 Sqn, and by the end of the war he had scored a total of ten victories, received the DFC and been made a captain.

Born on 9 June 1898, Lt Norman William Hustings came from Everton, Liverpool. He joined No 19 Sqn in the autumn of 1917, and gained his first victory flying a SPAD VII. In the first half of 1918, and now at the controls of a Dolphins, Hustings brought his tally of claims to seven before being rested – five of his kills were made flying C3899. He remained in the service after the war, before being transferred to the Class 'A' Reserve in November 1922. Hustings was killed in a car accident the following April, whilst living in Wendover, Buckinghamshire.

The third Canadian ace from Toronto to serve with No 19 Sqn, Lewis Hector Ray had joined the RFC in Canada and attended the flying course at No 4 School of Military Aeronautics in his home city between May and December 1917. Securing his 'wings' flying Curtiss JN4s, he sailed for England, where he duly completed his training with No 91 Sqn before joining No 19 Sqn in France on 2 April 1918.

Ray's first three victories were all Pfalz scouts, which he claimed whilst flying Dolphin C4129. On 27 September he was credited with four victories (three Fokker biplanes and a kite balloon), which brought his final tally to seven. Ray was awarded the Order of Michael the Brave, 3rd Class, by Romania, which was gazetted in July 1919. One month after receiving this award, he left the RAF and returned home. Edgar Peatfield had been his mechanic;

No 19 Sqn's Lt Finley McQuiston DFC claimed nine of his ten victories whilst flying the Dolphin

Canadian Lt L H Ray scored three of his seven Dolphin victories in this machine (C4129 'R'), while fellow No 19 Sqn ace Lt C V Gardner claimed the first of his ten with it

Pilots of No 19 Sqn relax between patrols at Savy in the spring of 1918. They are, from left to right, Lt J A Aldridge, Capt R A Del'Haye, Lt C Montgomery-Moore and Capt J W Crane. Aldridge scored five victories, Del'Haye nine and Montgomery-Moore and Crane four apiece. The Dolphin parked behind them is C8087 'G', which had the word *INK* painted inside the 'G' to read *GINK*. This machine was flown by ten-kill ace Capt C V Gardner in August 1918

'I knew Hector Ray very well, and I was his engine mechanic for practically the whole time he was with us until I was made the flight commander's mechanic. Ray was a very nice chap, and very interesting to talk to. He had been an agent for Standard Cars in Canada, and I well remember that his machine had a very good engine. In fact Maj Sanday had ruled that after doing 200 hours (I believe) all engines had to be taken out and thoroughly overhauled. Well, C4129 was running so well that Ray personally asked the new CO (Pretyman) if he could keep it so long as it ran okay, and the CO agreed. I never knew the CO grant anyone else such consent. I remember that this machine was letter "R", and when our rigger asked Ray was it because of his name, Ray said that it stood for a buckshee nigger named Rastus!'

Another youngster with the unit was John Arthur Aldridge from Twickenham, Middlesex. Born on 9 February 1899 (like Ray, he too was just 19), he had been a clerk with the civil service (Agricultural and Fisheries Department) between 1914-17, and as soon as he was old enough he had enlisted in the Oxford and Bucks Light Infantry in February 1917. After attending the 6th Officer's Cadet Battalion as a private, Aldridge had transferred to the RFC in April 1917, aged just 18. Commissioned on 23 May, he went to No 19 Sqn in January 1918 after completing his training.

Aldridge downed his first German on 21 April, and between then and September, he claimed a total of five victories, all in C3833, before returning to Home Establishment (England) on 2 October. He was awarded the Belgian CdG and left the RAF in January 1919.

Yet another 19-year-old was Arthur Winston Blake, born on 13 December 1898. A farmer from the Transvaal, in South Africa, he joined the RFC in August 1917 while still 18. His five victories were scored between May and the end of July, three of them in C3796. After the war he returned home and joined the South African Air Force, but he was killed in a flying accident on 14 December 1922 when his DH 9 was caught in a whirlwind at Dealsville, in Orange Free State.

A flight commander who so nearly became an ace on Dolphins was Capt Patrick Huskinson MC. He was the pilot who had chased the Gotha bombers while testing the Dolphin back in December 1917 (see Chapter 1). Born on 17 March 1896 and educated a Harrow School, he went into the Royal Military College at Sandhurst, and after service in the army transferred to the RFC from the Notts & Derby Regiment in 1915. Huskinson flew with No 2 Sqn in 1916, during which time he was awarded his MC, and in 1917 he was transferred to No 19 Sqn. He claimed seven victories flying the SPAD VII and four more in Dolphin C3792 – this success resulted in him receiving a Bar to his MC.

In 1919 Huskinson commanded No 70 Sqn in Germany, and he remained in the RAF post-war, eventually commanding RAF Station North Coates in 1936. During World War 2 he was blinded during an air raid, but he remained in the service and helped to develop the RAF's 4000-lb block-buster bomb. Huskinson was appointed CBE in 1942, and received the American Legion of Merit in 1945 as an air commodore. He died in November 1966.

No 79 Sqn

Lt E W Lees claimed No 79 Sqn's first victory during an afternoon patrol on 23 March 1918 when he downed a two-seater in flames over Nesle at 1645 hrs – this was probably a machine from ground support unit *Schutzstaffel* (*Schusta*) 31. Its next claim was made by Capt C Faber on 22 April, when he forced a Pfalz D III to crash. Faber was then hit by ground fire and wounded, however.

Capt William Mays Fry MC was the next to score, the ten-kill ace claiming his eleventh, and last, victory when he downed a Fokker Dr I on 11 May. 'Willie' Fry wrote this about the Dolphin in his book *Air of Battle* (William Kimber, 1974) while I was in correspondence with him;

'The Dolphin was a strongly built machine with a deep fuselage and greater wingspan than any scout which I had previously flown, having two pairs of wing struts each side. The wings had a slight back stagger and the pilot sat with his head sticking out of or just level with the top centre section, which was a hollow frame of steel tubing.

'The aeroplane came fitted with four machine-guns – two Vickers on the top of the engine, firing through the propeller, and two Lewis guns fixed one either side of the centre section, firing forward and upwards at an angle of about 45 degrees to the line of flight and over the propeller tips. Most of us discarded these Lewis guns at once as being of no use. The engine was the geared drive 220-hp Hispano-Suiza.

'Immediately I took the Dolphin into the air one could tell that it was a charming machine to fly, with no vices. It had excellent controls, and everything in the cockpit was in a handy position. One could also feel how strongly it was built. Although no one told us so at the time, and we had to find out for ourselves, the aeroplane had obviously been built with a view to operating at considerably greater heights than had hitherto been regarded as the norm. Its performance at 15,000 ft was far better than anything in my experience.

'One of the first things I found out was that we were expected to stay up longer on patrol, the Dolphin having greater petrol capacity and longer endurance, and that we were expected to escort bomber and reconnaissance formations for longer distances over any part of the front.'

No 79 Sqn's Lt F I Lord DFC poses with C3944 'N'. American Fred Lord achieved 12 victories in 1918, although this Dolphin only lasted until 2 May

A true adventurer, Capt Fred I Lord DFC saw further action in Russia in 1919 and then in Spain during the Civil War

On 20 May, No 79 Sqn CO Maj M W Noel claimed a hostile machine, but Capt H P Rushforth was forced to land at Wippenbach, inside British lines. The first claim by a squadron pilot who would later become an ace was made on 28 May by Lt F I Lord. He downed a balloon in flames at 0730 hrs near Comines in C4182.

Frederic Ives Lord was to enjoy an eventful life. Born in the American state of Wisconsin on 19 April 1900, he doctored his birth certificate (to show the year of his birth as 1894) so that he could join the military. Lord signed up with the 3rd Texas Infantry before being found out, so he set off for Canada to join the RFC instead. This time he succeeded, and when he arrived in France in March 1918 to serve with No 79 Sqn he was still only 17! Despite his youth, Lord proved a successful fighter pilot, downing 11 German aircraft following his balloon kill on 28 May. His run of success came to an end on 17 October when he was wounded. By then Lord had received the DFC and become a flight commander.

There was another Lord serving with No 79 Sqn in Germany at the end of the war, and he is sometimes confused with the American ace, especially in photographs.

Upon his release from hospital in March 1919, Lord volunteered for service in Russia, and he was given the job of commanding the RAF base at Pinega, as well as flying RE 8 two-seaters. Here, he received a Bar to his DFC, as well as two Russian decorations (the Order of St Anne with Swords and Bow, and the Stanislav Order with Swords and Bow), before leaving the service in order to return home to America. The Bar was for attacking Red (Bolshevik) troop columns from a height of 200 ft and stampeding horse traffic, which caused the break down of an expected attack on the White Russian positions. Oddly enough, this action took place on 27 June 1919, exactly one year to the day after Lord had downed three of his World War 1 combat victories in a single action in 1918.

Lord got his RE 8 back to base following this sortie, but it had a two-foot hole burned in one wing, a shot through main spar and longeron, an oil tank that had had one side blown out and a holed fuel tank. The bullet holes in the rest of the machine were too numerous to even count.

Back in the US, Lord became a 'barn-stormer', then began a flying service between San Antonio, Texas and Monterray, in Mexico (Linea Aerea), and it is thought he gave flight instruction to members of the Mexican Air Force, as well as being an adviser to Mexico during the 1929 Revolution. Lord also instructed at Floyd Bennet Field for the US Army Air Corps, holding the rank of major in the Reserve.

He flew Bréguet 19s in the Spanish Civil War on the Republican side, and at the start of World War 2 it is understood that he tried to use his false (now corrected?) birth certificate to rejoin the RAF. Indeed, the story goes that Lord actually managed to rejoin his old No 79 Sqn, now

Also an American, Lt F W Gillet DFC claimed 20 victories between August and November 1918 flying with No 79 Sqn. This haul made him the most successful Dolphin pilot of the war

equipped with Hawker Hurricanes, before authority and bureaucracy caught up with him. He therefore flew and worked on Atlantic Air Ferry duties, bringing aircraft to England.

Frederic Lord was killed by a vagrant in California in 1967, a tragic and senseless end to this man who lusted for adventure and found it in full measure.

The top Dolphin ace of the war was also an American, and he too served with No 79 Sqn. Frederick Warrington Gillet was born in Baltimore, Maryland, on 28 November 1895, and nicknamed 'Razors', he served initially with the US Army Signal Corps. Here, he received flight training, before moving to Canada to join the RFC because US rules stated that he was too young to be commissioned. Completing his training in England, Gillet arrived on No 79 Sqn on 29 March 1918, but it was not until 3 August that he made his first kill, and like Frederic Lord, it was a kite balloon, flamed north of Estaires.

Gillet's first German aircraft went down on 18 August, and between then and the end of the war he accounted for 17 aircraft and three balloons, all claimed as destroyed – no 'out of control' victories. This score brought him a DFC and Bar, to which he added the Belgian CdG and the US Distinguished Service Medal. After the Armistice he returned home, going into a variety of business ventures. Gillet was a president of a liquor firm, director of a bank and a director of an estate corporation. He died on 21 December 1969, aged 74.

Fred Gillet used Dolphin D3584 'V' to score four of his victories (*Bruce/Leslie collection*)

'Razors' Gillet claimed two of his kills in this machine (H7244) in October 1918. A rebuilt Dolphin, it is seen wearing the code letter 'S' whilst serving with No 79 Sqn in Germany post-war

No 79 Sqn also produced the second ranking Dolphin ace in Ronald Burns Bannerman from Dunedin, New Zealand. Born in Invercargill on 21 September 1890, he had joined the RFC in March 1917, although he had learnt to fly the previous December, and reached No 79 Sqn in the early summer of the following year. Bannerman began scoring in August 1918, and on the 29th of that month he 'made ace'. He would gain his 11th victory on his 28th birthday, and by war's end had scored a total of 17 kills, 16 of which were termed as destroyed. For these achievements Bannerman received the DFC and Bar. He returned to New Zealand, and post-war he rose to the rank of air commodore in the Royal New Zealand Air Force (RNZAF) and was made a CBE. He died on 2 August 1978.

John Harry McNeaney was the only Canadian to 'make ace' with No 79 Sqn. Born on 30 May 1897 in Jarvis, Ontario, he joined the RFC in May 1917, having left his home in Hamilton. In June 1918 McNeaney was wounded during a ground strafing attack, but he returned to the squadron once he had recovered. In the final weeks of the war he scored five victories (four in E4712), and all were deemed to have been destroyed. McNeaney was awarded the DFC at around this time. Taken ill in early 1919 whilst in Germany, possibly during the great 'flu epidemic', he died on 1 March of that year.

Second ranking Dolphin ace was No 79 Sqn's Lt R B Bannerman DFC, the New Zealander claiming 17 victories

The final pilot to achiveve 'acedom' with 79 Sqn was yet another American. Edgar Taylor hailed from Central Falls, Rhode Island, and he arrived on the squadron in April 1918. Like a number of Dolphin aces, he was a

No 79 Sqn pilots Lts P Hamilton and V Snyder and Capt Bannerman DFC stand in front of C4235 'R'. Note that the Dolphin boasts a head protection frame over the cockpit

slow starter, not gaining his first victory until early August. Taylor then took on the challenge of balloon busting, destroying four of these dangerous targets during the same month, but in gaining his last one near Sailly sur la Lys on the 24th, he was hit by ground fire and crashed mortally wounded. Just 20 years of age, Taylor died the next day of his injuries, possibly in German hands. He has no known grave. All five of Taylor's victories were scored in Dolphin D3727.

No 23 Sqn

After its initial re-equipment problems, No 23 Sqn at last gained its first official combat victory with the Dolphin on 30 May 1918 when Lt R A Way shot down a German aircraft which was seen to crash near Hamel. A two-seater was also sent down out of control by two other pilots during the same action.

Mention should be made, however, of an action that took place some ten days prior to this on 20 May, involving No 23 Sqn's Lt Carlton Aquilla Crysler, a Canadian from Welland, Ontario, although born in Delhi, India. The 19-year-old had been attacked by three Fokker Dr Is, and in the subsequent dogfight, witnessed by many Allied troops on the ground, he reportedly shot down a triplane before his own aircraft was set on fire. He then rammed a second Fokker, and both machines fell blazing. Men on the ground watched stunned as the Canadian jumped from his burning Dolphin while still 500 ft up. Crysler was buried where he fell, by the railway line north of Villers Bretonneux. A *Jasta* 6 pilot appears to have put in a claim for a 'Camel' at this time and place, although there are no recorded German losses for this action.

The unit's next two confirmed kills – Pfalz D IIIs – came on 3 June, and they were credited to pilots who would achieve (*text continues on page 46*)

Canadian Capt J H McNeaney DFC of No 79 Sqn scored five victories in the last weeks of the war, only to die in the influenza epidemic on 1 March 1919

Colour Plates

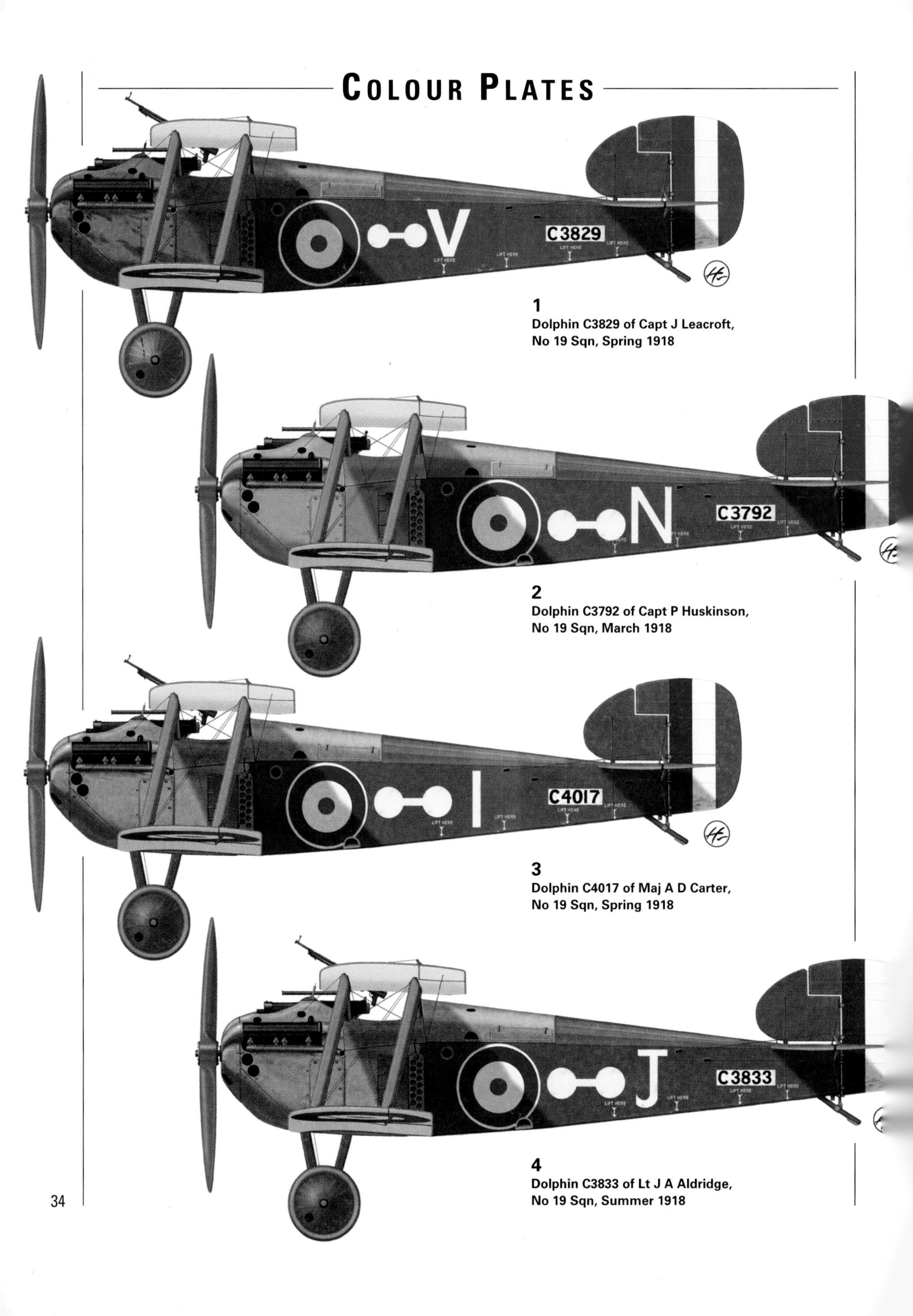

1
Dolphin C3829 of Capt J Leacroft, No 19 Sqn, Spring 1918

2
Dolphin C3792 of Capt P Huskinson, No 19 Sqn, March 1918

3
Dolphin C4017 of Maj A D Carter, No 19 Sqn, Spring 1918

4
Dolphin C3833 of Lt J A Aldridge, No 19 Sqn, Summer 1918

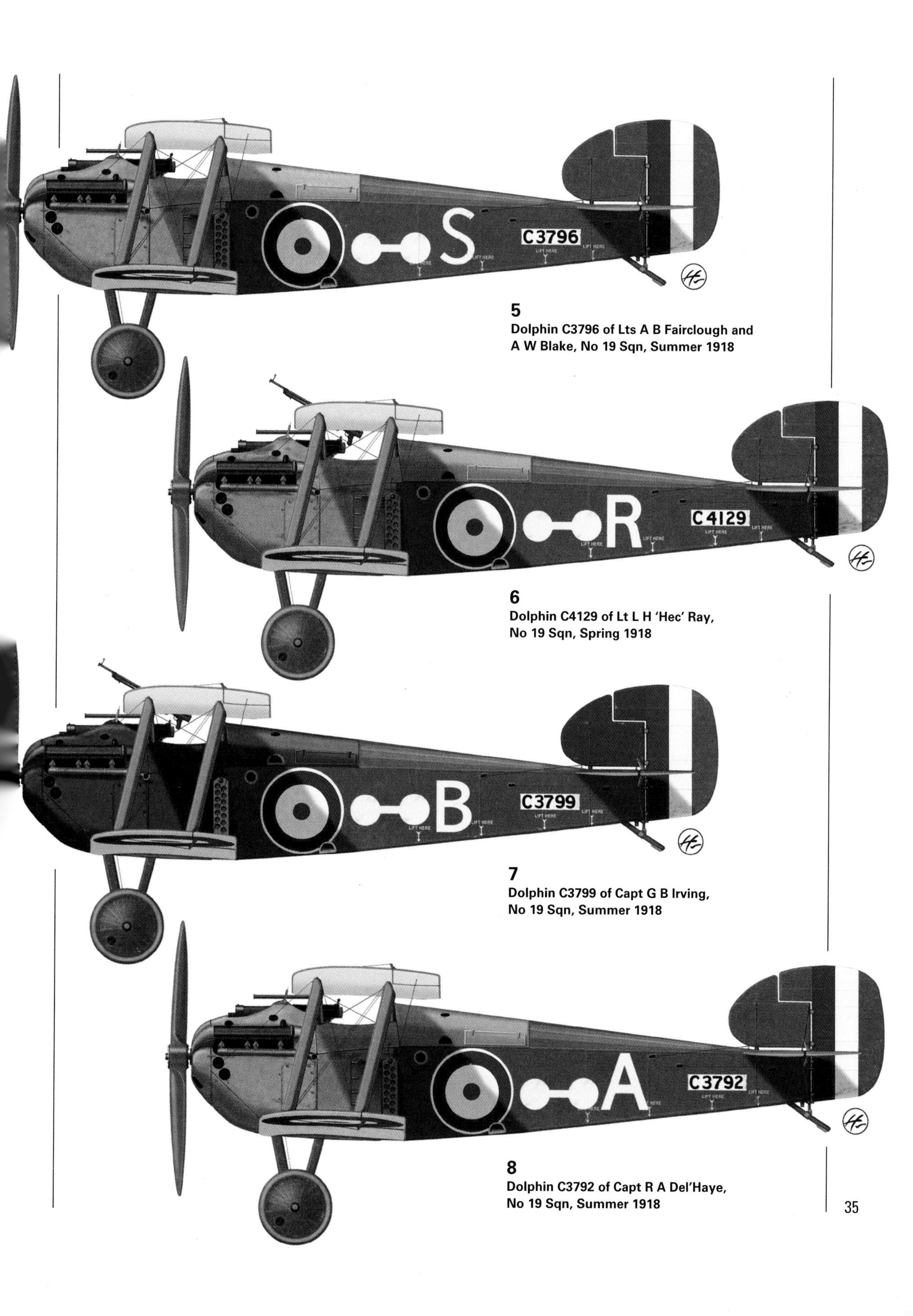

5
Dolphin C3796 of Lts A B Fairclough and A W Blake, No 19 Sqn, Summer 1918

6
Dolphin C4129 of Lt L H 'Hec' Ray, No 19 Sqn, Spring 1918

7
Dolphin C3799 of Capt G B Irving, No 19 Sqn, Summer 1918

8
Dolphin C3792 of Capt R A Del'Haye, No 19 Sqn, Summer 1918

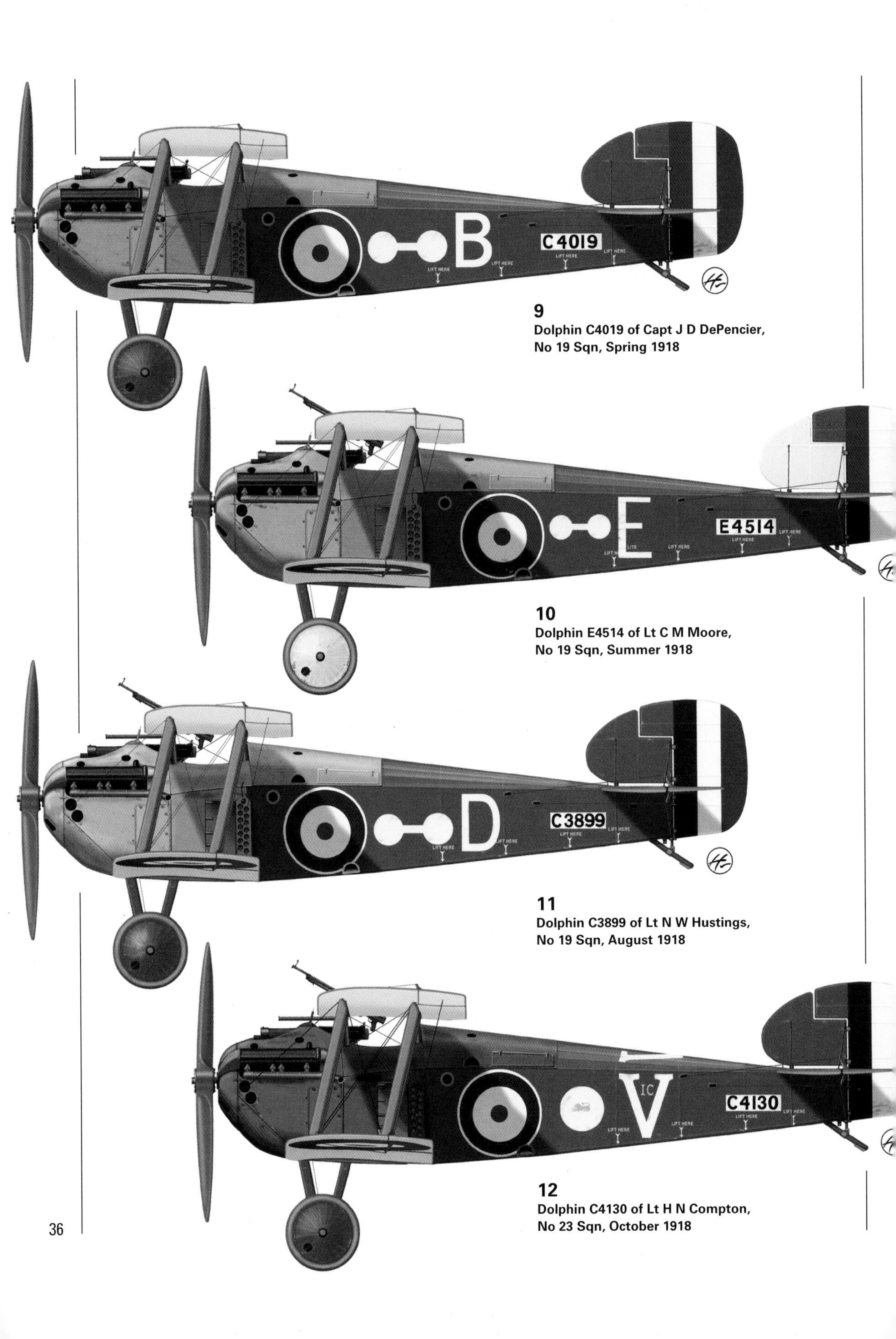

9
Dolphin C4019 of Capt J D DePencier, No 19 Sqn, Spring 1918

10
Dolphin E4514 of Lt C M Moore, No 19 Sqn, Summer 1918

11
Dolphin C3899 of Lt N W Hustings, No 19 Sqn, August 1918

12
Dolphin C4130 of Lt H N Compton, No 23 Sqn, October 1918

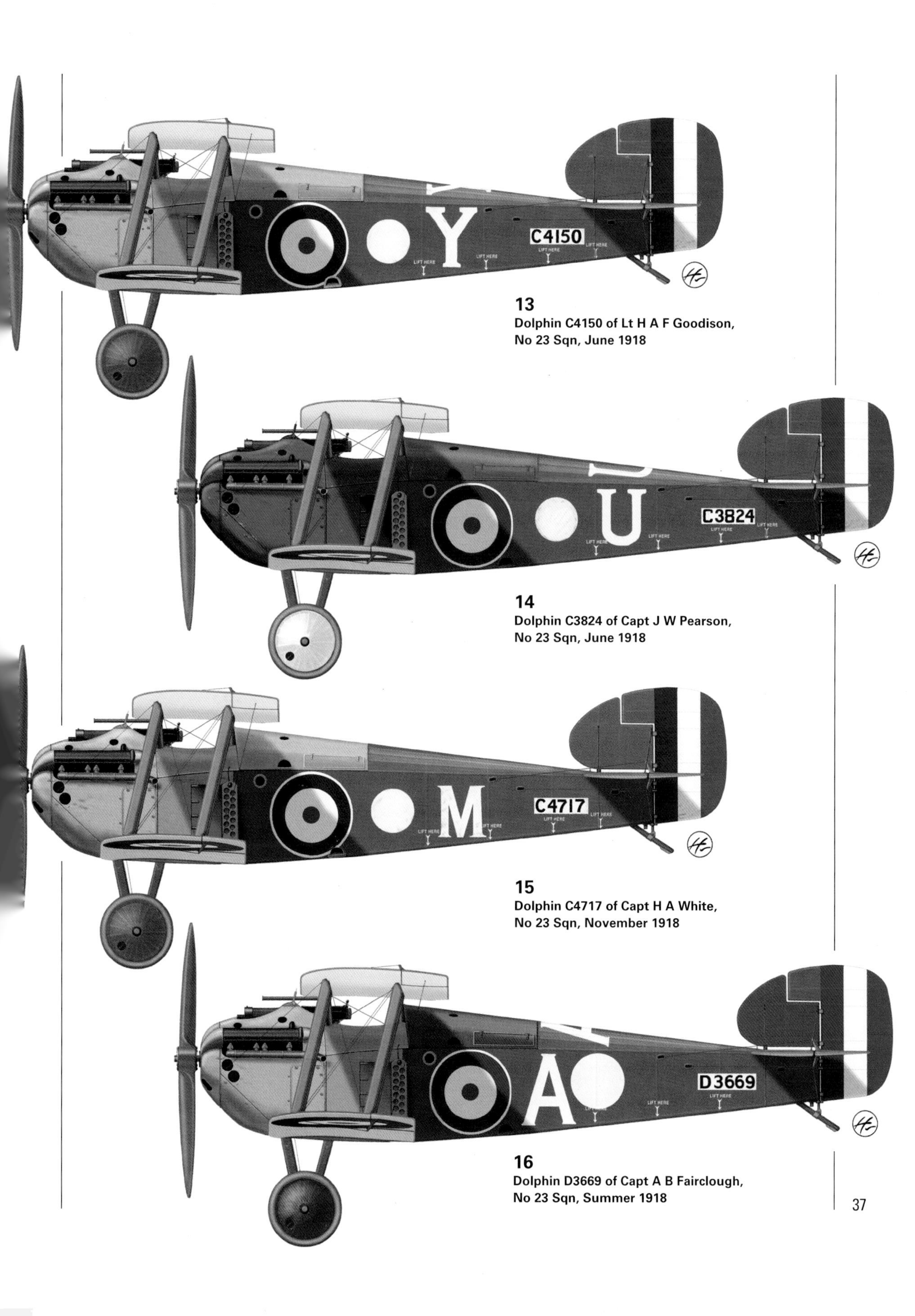

13
Dolphin C4150 of Lt H A F Goodison, No 23 Sqn, June 1918

14
Dolphin C3824 of Capt J W Pearson, No 23 Sqn, June 1918

15
Dolphin C4717 of Capt H A White, No 23 Sqn, November 1918

16
Dolphin D3669 of Capt A B Fairclough, No 23 Sqn, Summer 1918

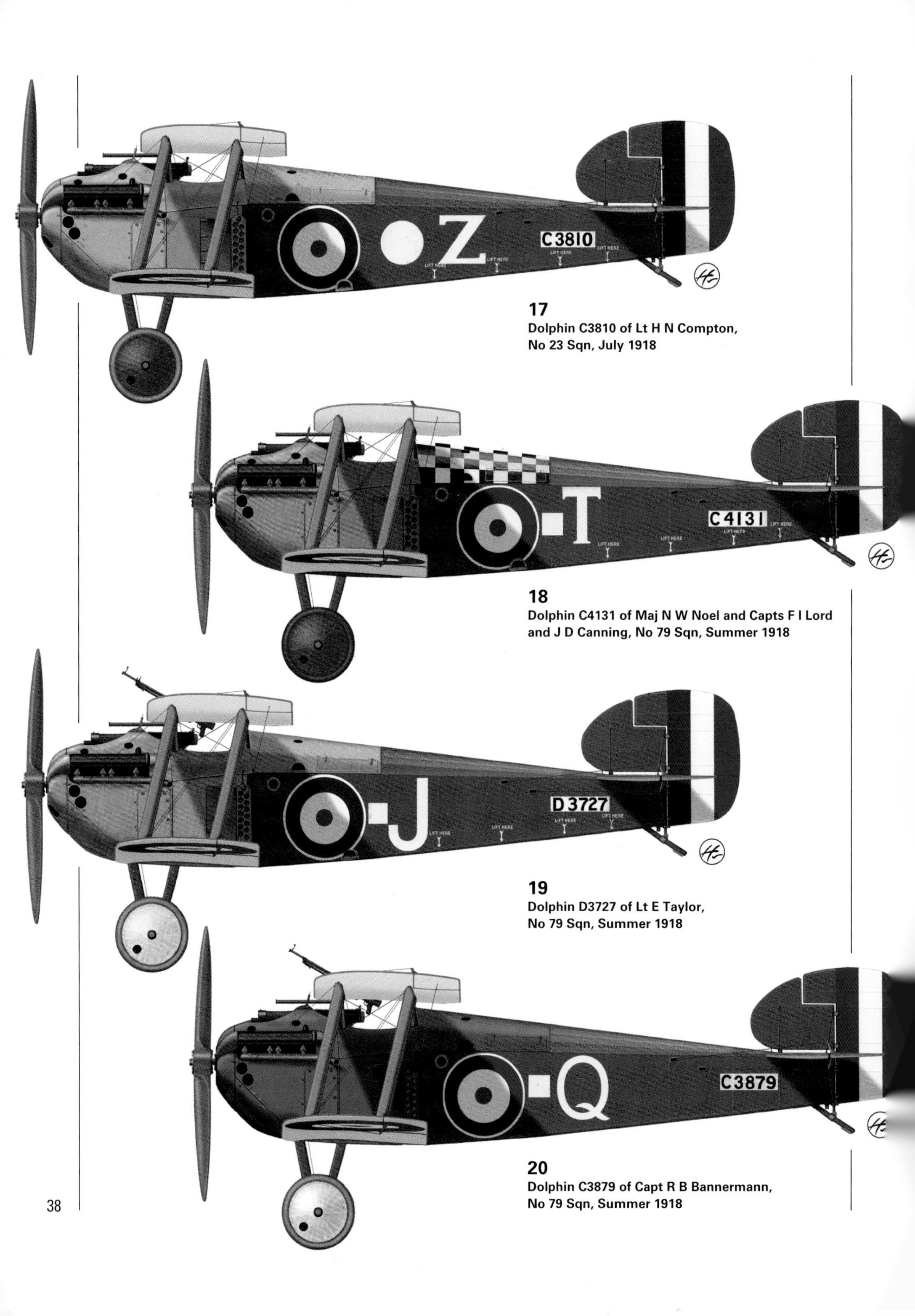

17
Dolphin C3810 of Lt H N Compton, No 23 Sqn, July 1918

18
Dolphin C4131 of Maj N W Noel and Capts F I Lord and J D Canning, No 79 Sqn, Summer 1918

19
Dolphin D3727 of Lt E Taylor, No 79 Sqn, Summer 1918

20
Dolphin C3879 of Capt R B Bannermann, No 79 Sqn, Summer 1918

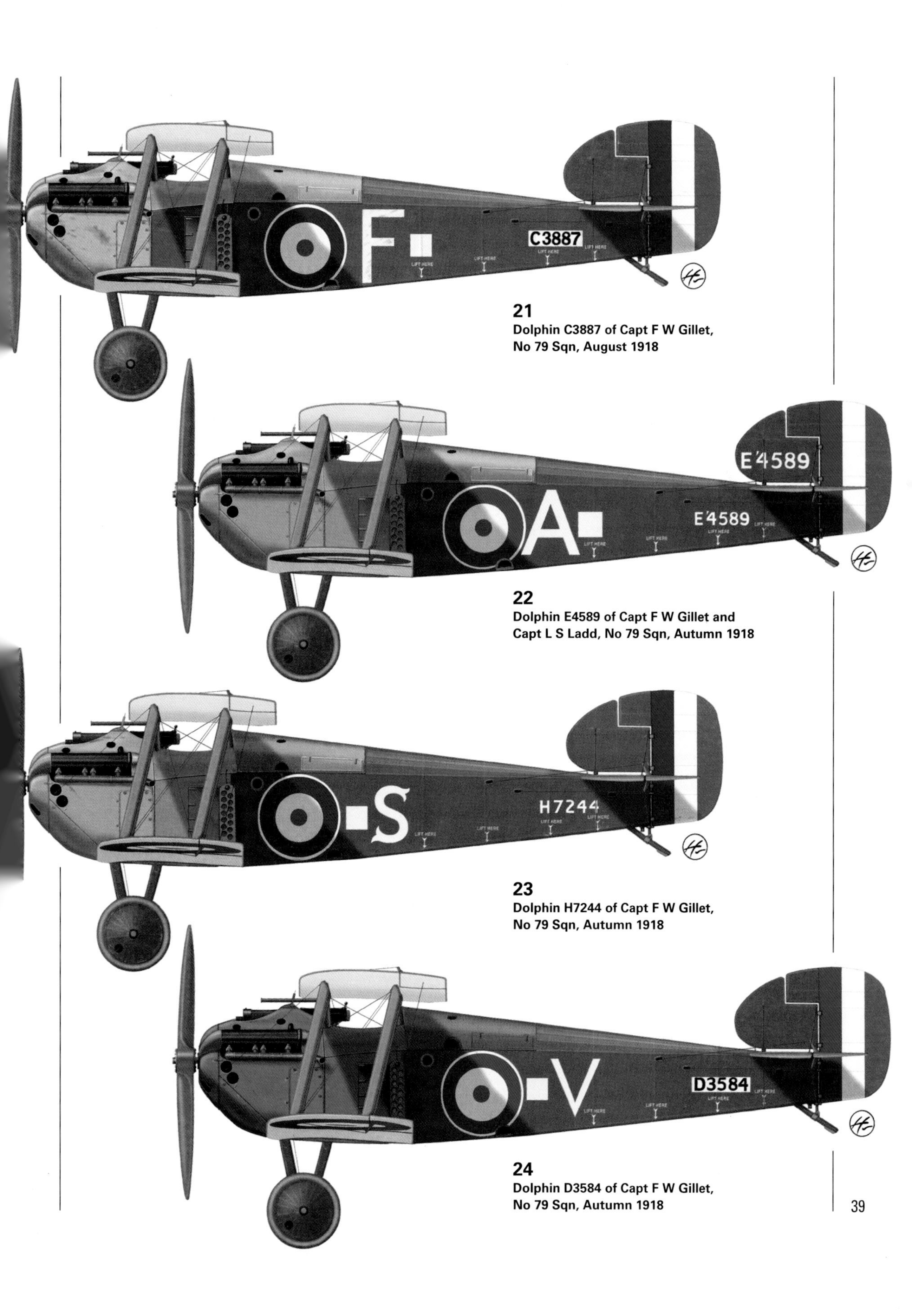

21
Dolphin C3887 of Capt F W Gillet, No 79 Sqn, August 1918

22
Dolphin E4589 of Capt F W Gillet and Capt L S Ladd, No 79 Sqn, Autumn 1918

23
Dolphin H7244 of Capt F W Gillet, No 79 Sqn, Autumn 1918

24
Dolphin D3584 of Capt F W Gillet, No 79 Sqn, Autumn 1918

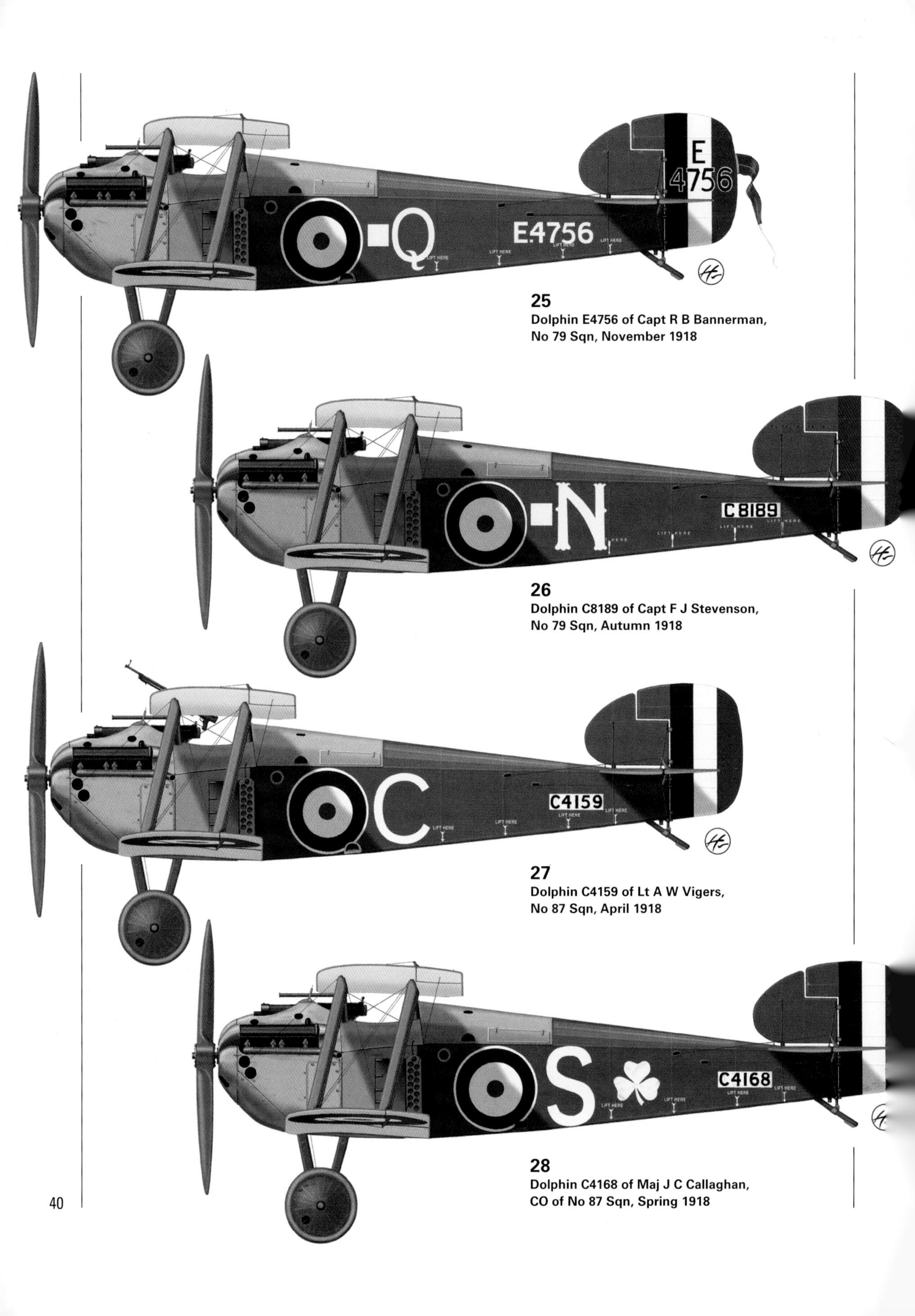

25
Dolphin E4756 of Capt R B Bannerman, No 79 Sqn, November 1918

26
Dolphin C8189 of Capt F J Stevenson, No 79 Sqn, Autumn 1918

27
Dolphin C4159 of Lt A W Vigers, No 87 Sqn, April 1918

28
Dolphin C4168 of Maj J C Callaghan, CO of No 87 Sqn, Spring 1918

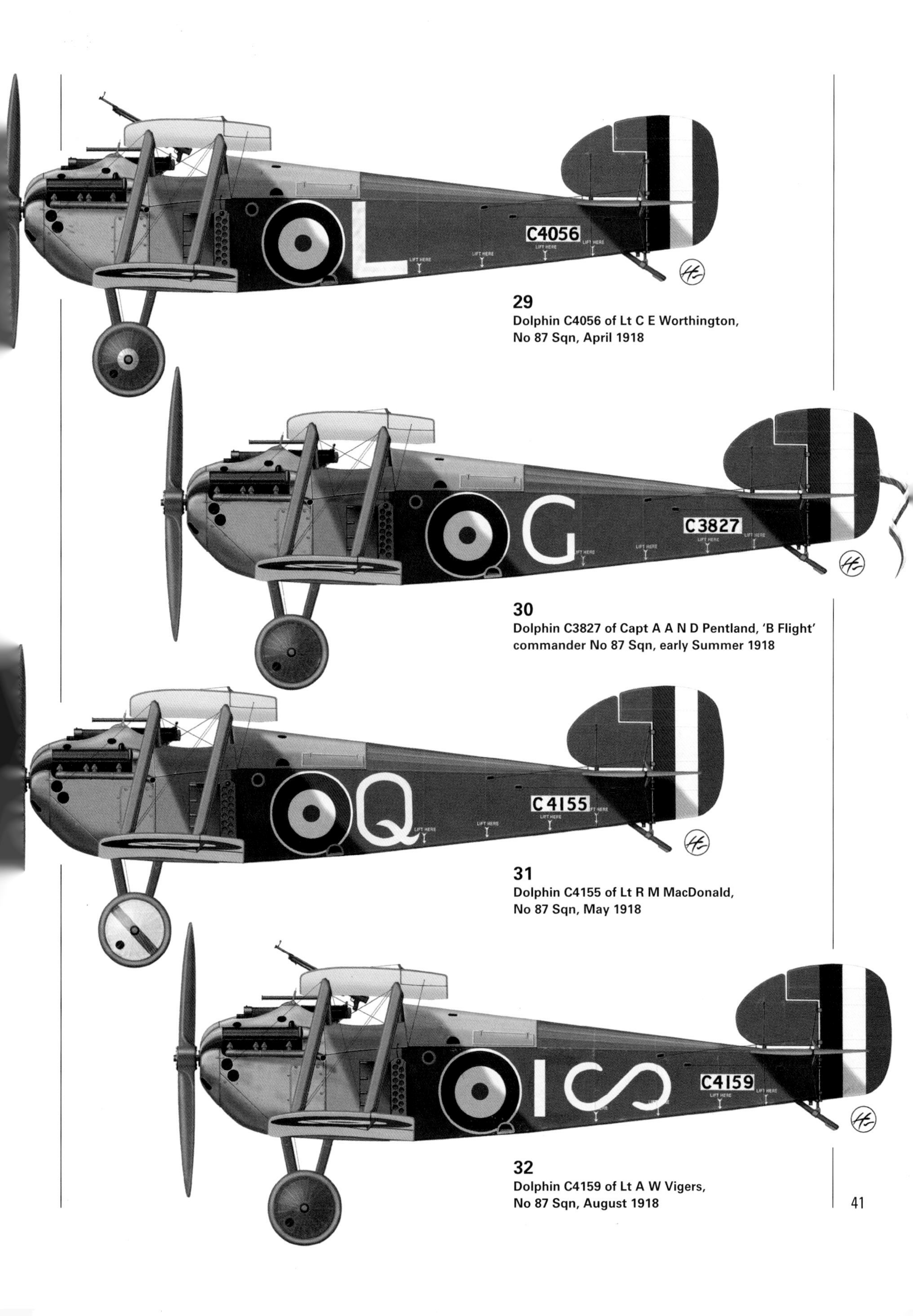

29
Dolphin C4056 of Lt C E Worthington, No 87 Sqn, April 1918

30
Dolphin C3827 of Capt A A N D Pentland, 'B Flight' commander No 87 Sqn, early Summer 1918

31
Dolphin C4155 of Lt R M MacDonald, No 87 Sqn, May 1918

32
Dolphin C4159 of Lt A W Vigers, No 87 Sqn, August 1918

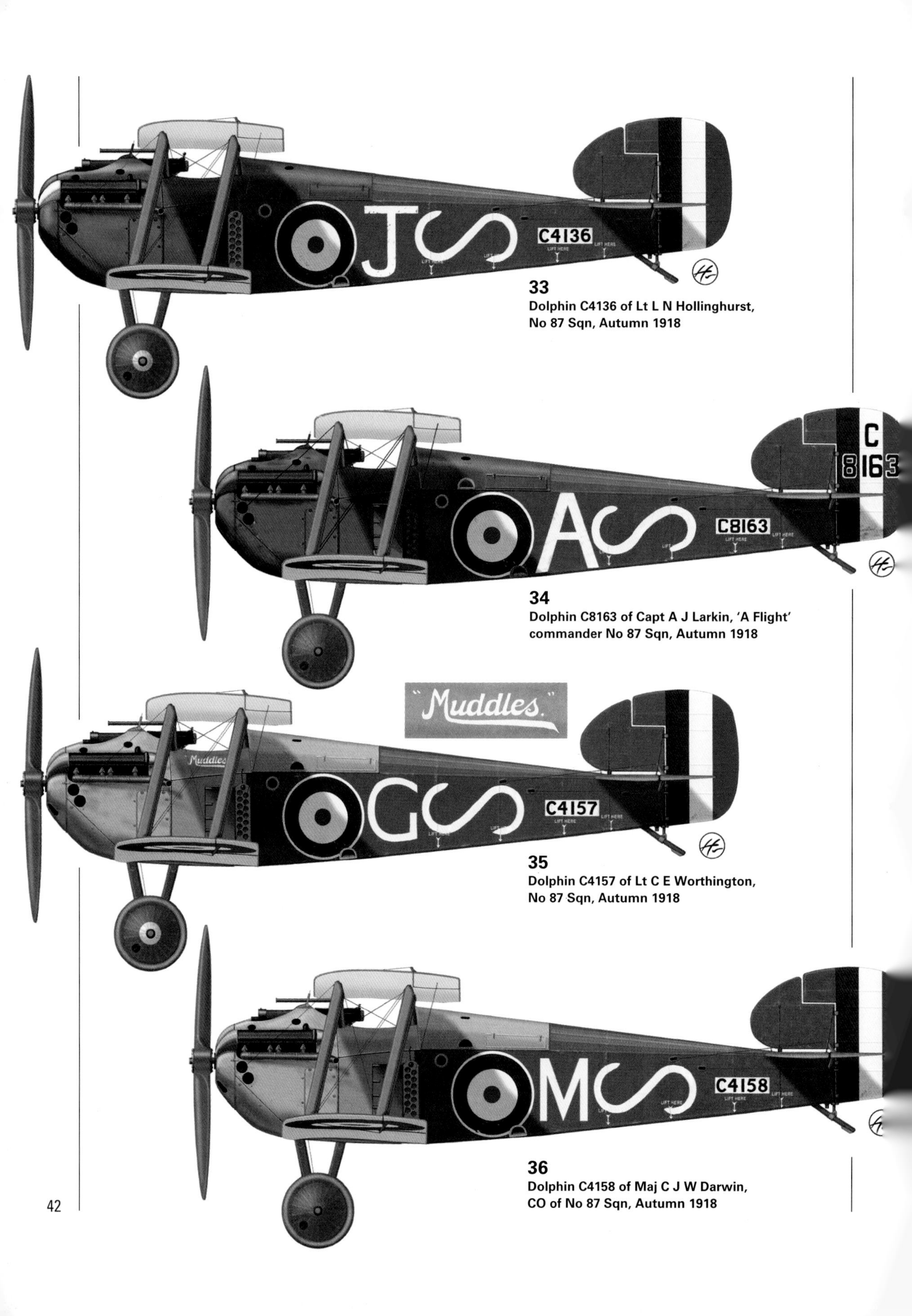

33
Dolphin C4136 of Lt L N Hollinghurst, No 87 Sqn, Autumn 1918

34
Dolphin C8163 of Capt A J Larkin, 'A Flight' commander No 87 Sqn, Autumn 1918

35
Dolphin C4157 of Lt C E Worthington, No 87 Sqn, Autumn 1918

36
Dolphin C4158 of Maj C J W Darwin, CO of No 87 Sqn, Autumn 1918

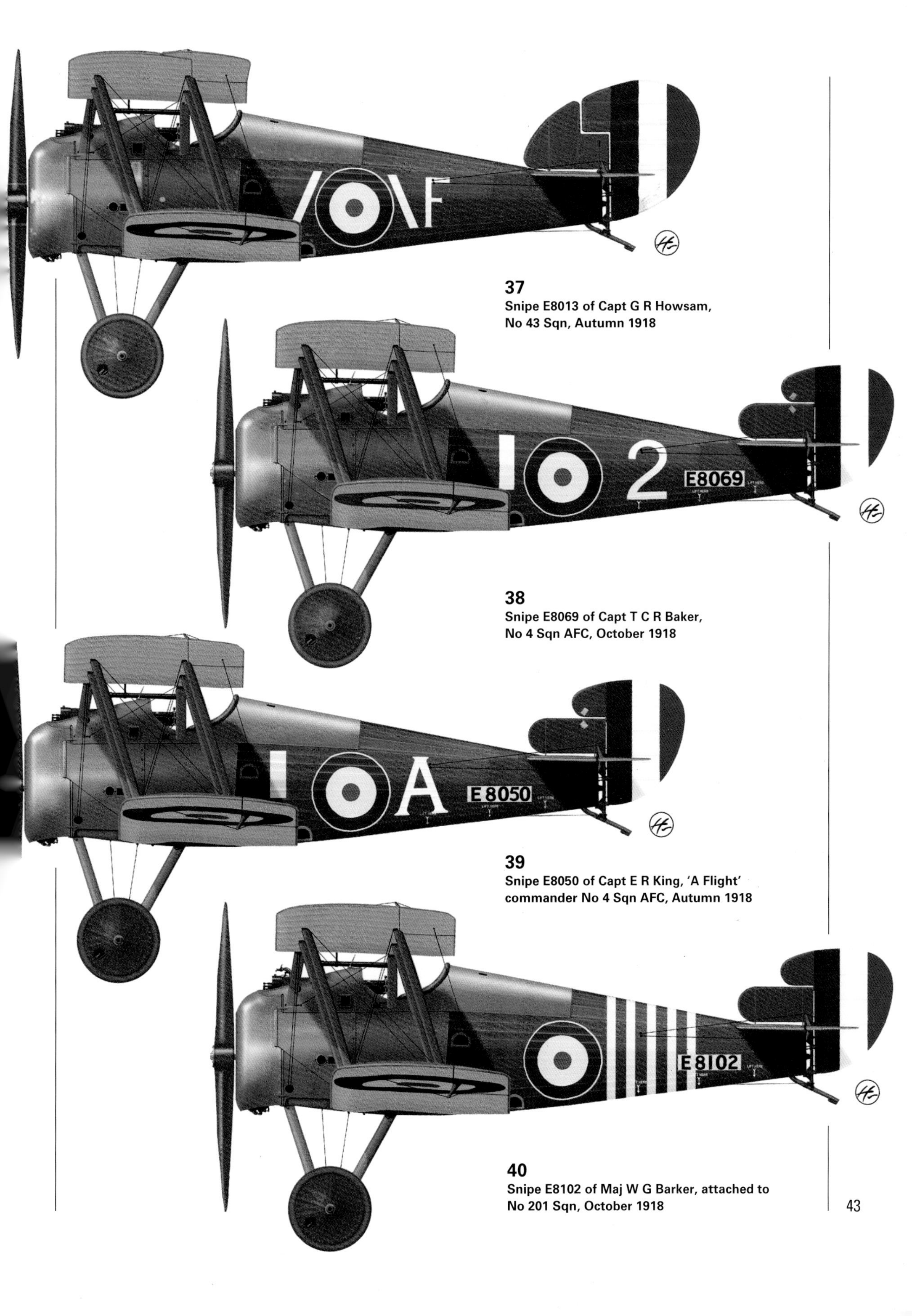

37
Snipe E8013 of Capt G R Howsam, No 43 Sqn, Autumn 1918

38
Snipe E8069 of Capt T C R Baker, No 4 Sqn AFC, October 1918

39
Snipe E8050 of Capt E R King, 'A Flight' commander No 4 Sqn AFC, Autumn 1918

40
Snipe E8102 of Maj W G Barker, attached to No 201 Sqn, October 1918

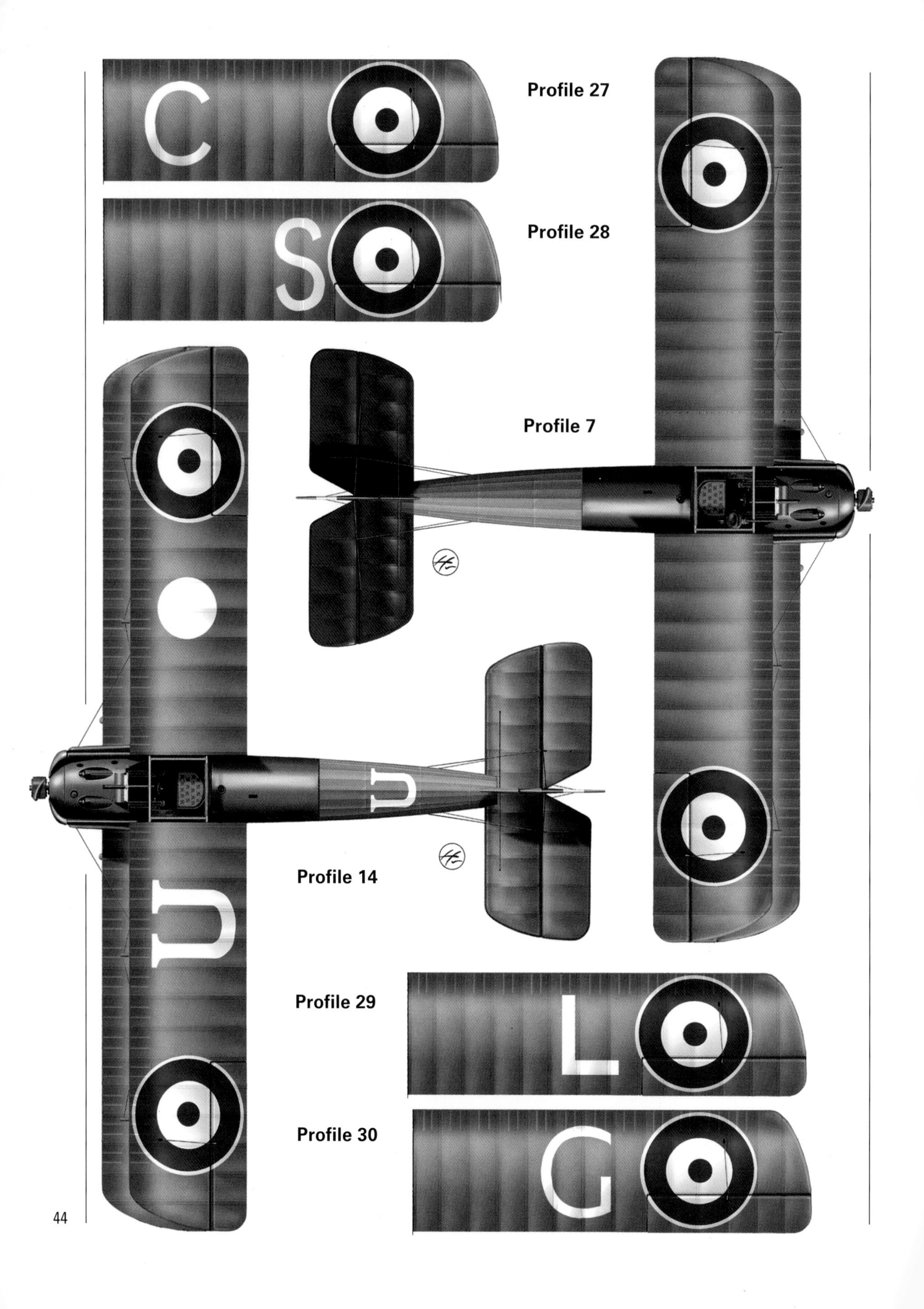
Profile 27
Profile 28
Profile 7
Profile 14
Profile 29
Profile 30

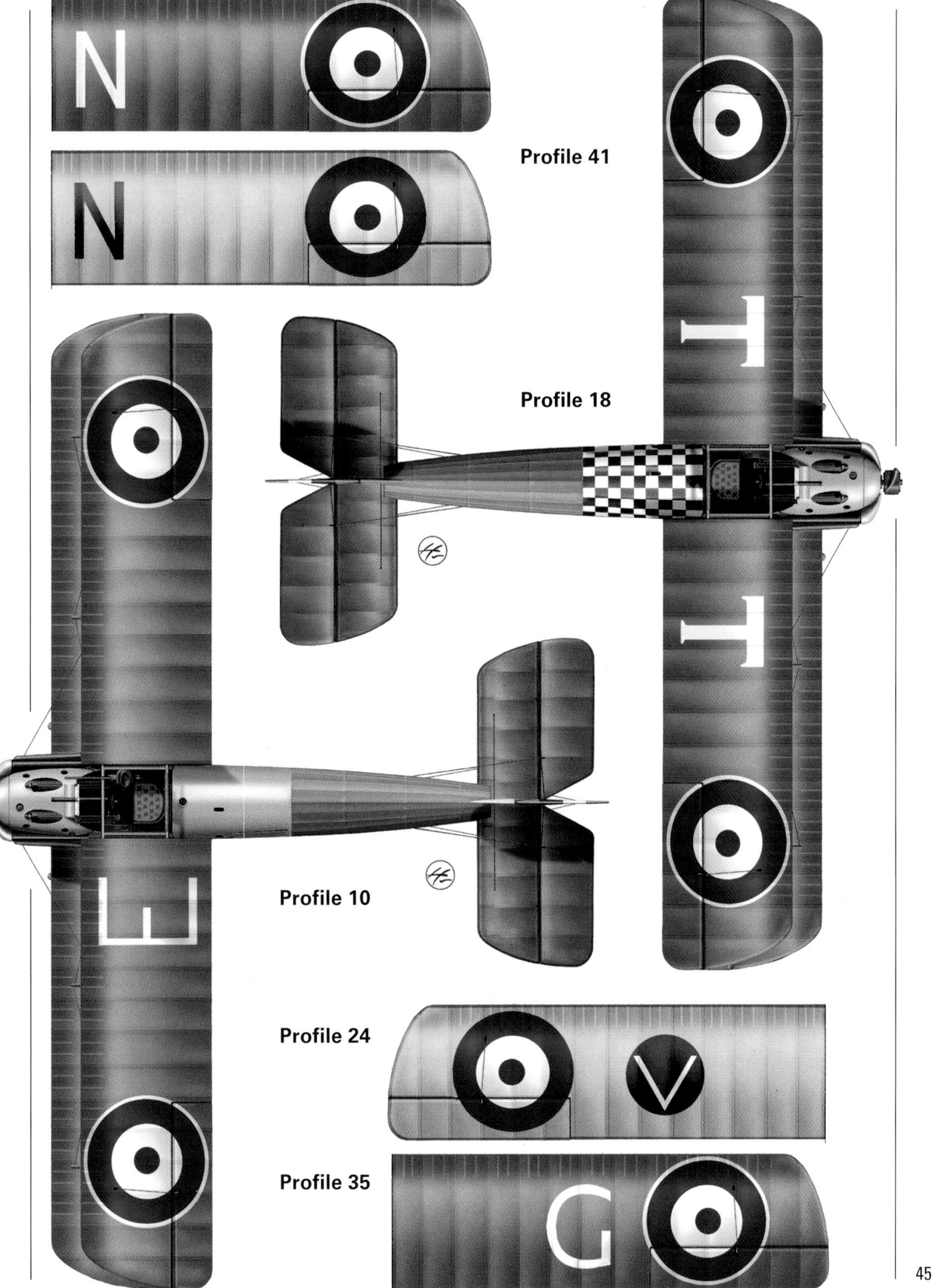
Profile 41
Profile 18
Profile 10
Profile 24
Profile 35

'acedom', Lts H A F Goodison and J W Pearson. One of the German pilots was from *Jasta* 79b, and he became a prisoner of war.

No 23 Sqn would produce four Dolphin aces, and have another claim his all important fifth victory after earlier claims flying the SPAD VII/XIII. The highest scorer of these was American James William Pearson. Born on 2 April 1895 in Bridgeport, Connecticut, he was living in Nutley, New Jersey, at the time he joined the RFC in Canada. Pearson worked for the General Electric Company in Hamilton, New Jersey, pre-war, the company making incandescent lamps. His flying course at No 4 School of Military Aeronautics (SMA) in Toronto ran from September to November 1917, after which he crossed the Atlantic to England, where he completed his training. Pearson arrived on No 23 Sqn just as it was changing over from SPAD XIIIs to Dolphins, and he was one of the two pilots to share the 'out of control' victory on 30 May, south of Albert. He next saw action on 3 June whilst patrolling the Montdidier-Vignieres-Contoir line between 1710-1740 hrs Pearson's combat report for this action reads:

'While on Offensive Patrol I saw a formation of Pfalz scouts in the neighbourhood of Montdidier. After some preliminary manoeuvring, our formation attacked. I singled out an EA and dived, firing a burst of about 100 rounds, closing the range to about 15 yards. I noticed smoke and then flames coming from its fuselage. I then zoomed away and saw the EA go down vertically, well on fire.'

After his Pfalz kill on 3 June. Pearson did not score again until 1 July, when he downed two Albatros scouts. He then endured a gap of another month before claiming his second double (a two-seater Halberstadt and another Pfalz) on 1 August. These kills made him an ace. Pearson broke part of this sequence by not claiming any victories on 1 September, but he was again credited with two kills on 18 September (two Fokker D VIIs), and another double on 28 October (two more Fokker biplanes).

The first Fokker on 18 September went down on fire, Pearson having intended to attack balloons, which meant he had Buckingham incendiary ammunition loading in his gun-belts. Attacking the D VII and seeing it begin to burn came as no surprise to him. His final two kills were credited on 29 October and 1 November, and both were two-seaters. The latter was a DFW C-type, which he engaged near Petit Beart at around noon, flying in company with Lts H N Compton (C4130) and E J Taylor (E4739);

'When on an Offensive Patrol, I saw a DFW about 1000 ft below. I dived, followed by Lts Compton and Taylor. I lost sight of the EA while diving, but eventually picked it up. We all attacked, firing simultaneously – I got to very close range before pulling out. The EA went down in a glide, eventually striking a tree with its left wing and crashing in a field. Lt Taylor finished up at about 500 ft from the ground, engaging enemy infantry and transport on the roads until his ammunition was used up.'

Jim Pearson had flown a variety of Dolphins, although his first four claims were made in C3824. Promoted to captain, he received the DFC for his 12 successes, while the French also presented him with the CdG. He left the RAF in September 1919, and like so many other airmen from this conflict, he then disappeared into obscurity as far as aviation was concerned. However, Pearson went into textiles, and began his own

American Capt J W Pearson DFC was No 23 Sqn's most successful Dolphin ace, claiming 12 kills in 1918

Five pilots from No 23 Sqn are seen at Berty East in late October 1918. They are, from left to right Capt J W Pearson and Lts J C Urquhart, J Mavity, C E Thomas and E J Taylor

successful business back in Nutley, New Jersey. He died at his home in Upper Montclair, New Jersey, on 28 January 1993, just short of his 98th birthday. At the time of his passing, Jim Perason is believed to have been the last surviving American ace from World War 1.

Harold Albert White, was yet another American Dolphin ace. 'Pete' White came from up-state New York, but gave his address as Branford, Ontario (that of a relative), upon joining the RFC in Canada in order to disguise his true nationality. Prior to joining up, he had been working for the Motor Truck Company. His flying course was also conducted at No 4 SMA in Toronto on the JN4, between September and November 1917. Soon after he arrived in England, White joined No 90 Sqn at Shotwick, near Chester, in March 1918, before being transferred to No 23 Sqn.

Upon his arrival in France, he was shocked to find the unit still flying SPAD XIIIs, but the delayed change to the Dolphin was soon made. Not the best of pilots, White crashed several Dolphins, and even put himself in hospital after smashing up the CO's machine on 24 May!

He received the DFC for his seven victories, scored between June and September 1918 – he may have also shot down a two-seater on 9 November, bringing his score to eight. The following combat report was lodged by White on 16 September following an Offensive Patrol and Escort mission flown at 0830 hrs for RAF bombers near St Quentin. He had already claimed one aircraft out of control with another pilot by the time this particular action took place;

'While on Offensive Patrol, I was leading the lower formation when we were attacked by a formation of about seven EA. A general engagement followed in which I singled out one and chased him down to about 7000 ft, firing three or four bursts from 50 to 25 yards' range. After the last burst the FEA, who had been "S" turning to avoid my fire, went into a vertical dive. Almost immediately a burst of black smoke came from the Fokker, which increased rapidly and in quantity. There is no doubt in my mind that the FEA was on fire. The last I saw of the EA was still going down vertically, emitting clouds of black smoke.'

Harry White left the squadron in January 1919, and he was lucky to survive a bout of Spanish 'flu during the world-wide pandemic. Once he had recovered, White returned home to Canada. Immediately after the war he tried his hand at 'barn-storming' in an old JN4 'Jenny', but when

American Capt H A 'Pete' White DFC also 'made ace' with No 23 Sqn in 1918 on the Dolphin, claiming seven kills

Dolphin E4717 'M' was flown by Capt H A White (seen here by the fighter's nose), and he claimed that it was 'the fastest machine on the squadron'

his money finally ran out, he returned to the family home in Schenectady, New York, at the end of 1919.

Canadian Harry Neville Compton was born in Winnipeg on 9 April 1899, although when he joined up he was living at Westholme on Vancouver Island, British Columbia. During 1915-16 he became a sergeant – aged just 16 or 17 – with the Canadian Royal Engineers, before transferring to the RFC in Canada on the last day of March 1917.

Commissioned in July, Compton sailed to England and then moved to France. Joining No 23 Sqn, the 19-year-old scored five victories, starting 1 July (an Albatros scout), and ending with a DFW two-seater shared with Pearson and Taylor on 1 November. He too received the DFC as a result of his successes in combat, before returning home to Westholme. He died in Toronto in 1951.

Mention was made earlier in the No 19 Sqn section of this chapter of Capt A B Fairclough MC, who had claimed nine victories in SPAD VIIs, followed by five on Dolphins. He was then tranferred to No 23 Sqn as a flight commander in May 1918, and before he was rested in July, he had downed a further five German aircraft to bring his overall score to 19. Oddly enough, Fairclough received no decoration for his ten Dolphin kills.

Only one No 23 Sqn pilot scored five victories flying both the SPAD and the Dolphin – 20-year-old Henry Arthur Frank Goodison. The son of a stockbroker, he came from Highgate, North London, and had been educated at Highgate School, where he was enrolled in the Officer Training Corps (OTC) prior to joining up. Goodison joined No 23 Sqn at the tail-end of its SPAD era, downing two German aircraft in March 1918. He shared these two victories with other pilots, and both aircraft were downed inside Allied lines – an Albatros D Va of *Jasta* 44s (a Saxon unit) on 18 March and an LVG two-seater five days later.Once flying the Dolphin, he increased his tally to five kills on 27 June before being rested. Goodison later flew as an instructor at No 204 Training Depot.

Capt Leslie Morton Mansbridge from Wales (born 13 June 1897) also claimed a number of victories using a French-built scout, before downing his all important fifth kill in a No 23 Sqn Dolphin. A former army man, he had scored four victories with No 1 Sqn flying Nieuports before being

Canadian Capt H N Compton DFC scored five kills with No 23 Sqn between July and November 1918 (*via S K Taylor*)

Lt Harry Compton used Dolphin C4130 'V' to down his last two victories

Lt Harry Compton prepares to leave on a patrol from Bertry East in late October 1918. This aircraft is almost certainly C4130 'V'

wounded on 3 June 1917. Upon his recovery, Mansbridge had gone to No 23 Sqn as a flight commander, and on 22 April 1918 he sent a Fokker Dr I down 'out of control' for his fifth, and last, victory. He died in 1993.

No 87 Sqn

Once this new outfit had received its second batch of Dolphins after having had to give its first consignment to No 23 Sqn, No 87 Sqn finally flew to France on 25 April 1918. Led by one of the RAF's more extrovert squadron commanders, Maj J C 'Casey' Callaghan MC, the unt boasted three experienced flight commanders and a host of enthusiastic embryo pilots, some of whom had been observers before earning their 'wings'.

Lt H A F Goodison became an ace with two SPAD and three Dolphin victories whilst flying with No 23 Sqn in 1918

Lt Henry Goodison got two of his three Dolphin kills in this machine, C4150 'Y'. It had been issued to No 23 Sqn on 29 June 1918 (*Bruce/Leslie collection*)

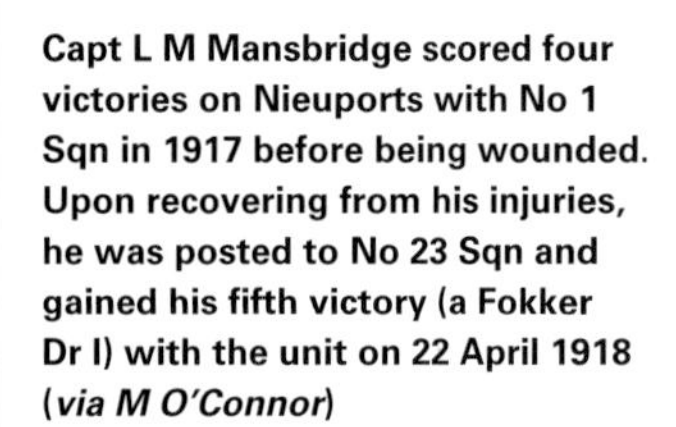

Capt L M Mansbridge scored four victories on Nieuports with No 1 Sqn in 1917 before being wounded. Upon recovering from his injuries, he was posted to No 23 Sqn and gained his fifth victory (a Fokker Dr I) with the unit on 22 April 1918 (*via M O'Connor*)

The unit set up at Petite Synthe, near Dunkirk, prior to moving to Estrée-lés-Crécy to begin operational flying in May. No 87 Sqn scored its first victory on 6 May, when a Rumpler two-seater was downed in flames by Lt H A R Biziou, although he subsequently force landed (his Dolphin turned over) after the sortie, surviving without injury. 'Weegee' Biziou completed the following combat report of his action against the Rumpler – which he described as having a partly red fuselage – over Gheluvelt at 1740 hrs;

'While on patrol with Capt Pentland we saw two EA about 3000 ft under us being "archied" (fired on by AA guns). We circled round them and dived on them from the sun. At 200 yards' range I opened fire on one and followed him down, firing all the time. At about 3000 ft he started to emit smoke and finally crashed completely. My engine choked on opening her out, and I only got it again after my wheels had touched the ground.'

The unit's next three claims came on 16 May, with Lts B Ankers, C E Worthington and E B Crickmore downing three Albatros scouts near Ostend in a fight with German Marine fighters, who had two of their

Brand new Dolphins of No 87 Sqn are seen lined up at Hounslow in early 1918. Aircraft 'S' (second from right) was assigned to squadron CO, Maj J C Callaghan. The fighter parked closest to the camera is C4173 'A', which was flown by Australian Capt H J Larkin. The future 11-kill ace claimed his first two victories with this machine on 3 June 1918

pilots wounded. Burton Ankers DCM (Distinguished Conduct Medal) had been CO Callaghan's observer earlier in the war, and now a pilot, he had got himself into Callaghan's new unit. Worthington would become and ace, while Canadian Crickmore became a prisoner of war in July after being shot down by a *Jasta* 46 pilot.

No 87 Sqn's 'ace of aces' was Arthur Whitehair Vigers, known as 'Wiggy'. Born on 20 January 1890, he had already been awarded the MC during his service with the Royal Engineers in 1915, as well as being Mentioned in Despatches. Vigers had then flown as an observer with No 15 Sqn prior to becoming a pilot. His first kill (a Fokker Dr I) came on 3 June, and his fifth on 10 August – on the latter occasion he downed three Fokker biplanes in as many minutes. Eleven days later Vigers 'bagged' two more over Biefvillers at 1745 hrs flying C4159;

'While on patrol, I became detached from the formation and followed Maj Darwin. At 5.45 pm we were at 18,000 ft near Bapaume, and dived on 14 Fokker biplanes at about 12,000 ft. I saw Maj Darwin attack a machine in the rear of the formation, which he shot down, and it crashed

Another view of No 87 Sqn Dolphins lined up at Hounslow in the early months of 1918. Aircraft 'L' (C4056) was assigned to Lt C E Worthington, and he scored his first of five victories with it on 16 May 1918. All 'B Flight' aircraft had a small white circle painted in the centre of the wheel cover (as seen here). Parked next to 'L' is C4162 'H', which was damaged in a crash on 4 September. By then, however, its pilots had scored three victories, including two to ace Capt A A N D Pentland MC

This photo of Maj Callaghan's C4168 reveals its decoration with a shamrock, denoting the pilot's Irish ancestry. Note that the letter 'S' was repeated on the top starboard wing (*Bruce/Leslie collection*)

A 14-kill ace, Capt A W Vigers MC DFC was No 87 Sqn's 'C Flight' commander from August 1918 until war's end. He is seen here whilst serving with the RAAF in the early 1920s

Capt Vigers' modified Dolphin (C4159) was photographed at Boussiéres in November 1918. Note that it has an experimental fit of two Lewis guns on the bottom lower wings, which were fired by a cable that ran from the cockpit. Neither gun had an ammunition drum in place when this photo was taken, and of course these could not be replaced in the air. C4159 '1' (formally 'C') was almost certainly the RAF's most successful Dolphin, with its various pilots claiming 15 victories whilst at the controls of the veteran fighter

west of Favreuil (this was Darwin's fourth kill). I dived on one which was firing on Maj Darwin, and stalling, he went into a vertical dive, and I fired about 50 more rounds at him and saw him crash just west of the Bapaume-Ervillers road. About 20 minutes later, we engaged eight Fokker biplanes a little west of Biefvillers. I dived on one and fired about 100 rounds at fairly close range, and I saw him turn on his back and begin to spin. I then had a cross feed in the right-hand gun and a No 3 stoppage in the left, and did not follow him down, but he appeared out of control.'

Vigers remained with the unit until 1919, by which time he had become a flight commander and received both the DFC and a second Mention in Despatches. In all, he claimed 14 victories – all scored in C4159. Vigers emigrated to Australia after the war, and later served with the RAAF. He died in September 1968.

One of the most colourful characters in the RFC/RAF, as well as in No 87 Sqn, was Alexander Augustus Norman Dudley Pentland MC. A wild 23-year-old Australian from Queensland (where he was born on 5 August 1894, although he later lived in Gosford, New South Wales), Pentland served for two years with the citizens forces in Australia, before joining the 12th Australian Light Horse. He saw action with the latter regiment firstly in Egypt, and then Gallipoli, where he fought with a machine gun section.

Evacuated with enteric fever, Pentland transferred to the RFC in February 1916, and flew BE 2s with No 16 Sqn, during which time he and his observer shot down a Fokker Eindecker. Converting to single-seaters, he went to No 29 Sqn whilst they were still flying DH 2s, but on the last day of June 1916 he broke his right leg playing football, ending up in a Red Cross Auxiliary Hospital in Brighton, Sussex. Recovering, and being assigned as an instructor at Hendon for a while, Pentland was then posted to No 19 Sqn while it had SPADs, and in the summer of 1917 he increased his score to ten, and won the MC. On one flight the Australian actually had a British artillery shell pass through his fuselage without hitting anything vital!

Wounded by shrapnel over Zonnebeke on 26 September, he crashed into a shell hole in the frontline area. Scrambling clear, he had begun to make his way to British trenches when he hit in the right thigh by a bullet. However, in less than a month he was fit again for duty. Back in

Pilots of No 87 Sqn pose in front of Capt Pentland's C3827 'G' at Dunkirk in the early summer of 1918. Pentland claimed four victories in this machine in May-June. Note the flight commander's streamer affixed to the fighter's rudder. Australian Pentland is standing fifth from the left, and fellow ace Lt L N Hollinghurst is stood to his left

Capt A A N D Pentland MC DFC scored nine of his first ten kills flying SPAD VIIs with No 19 Sqn, and then claimed a further 13 in Dolphins with No 87 Sqn before being wounded on 25 August 1918. Born in Queensland, he was known as the 'Wild Australian'. Pentland is seen here wearing warm clothing, which was always donned prior to hunting high-flying Rumplers

Capt Leslie Hollinghurst DFC commanded the cadre of No 87 Sqn in late 1918 just before he moved as a flight commander to No 79 Sqn in Germany. Note the early style of DFC ribbon below his 'wings', with its horizontal purple stripe rather than the now familiar diagonal striped ribbon

England, Pentland went to No 56 Training Squadron at London Colney, before being posted to No 87 Sqn.

As 'B Flight' Commander with his new unit, Pentland added a further 13 victories to his tally and received the DFC. Particularly aggressive, and a good flight commander, his war came to a premature end when he was wounded on 25 August in a fight with *Jasta* 57. Post-war, he served with the RAAF for a time, and then became a freelance pilot flying around the New Guinea gold fields. In 1930 he joined Australian National Airways, and in World War 2 he ran an air-sea rescue unit in the South Pacific with the RAAF, holding the rank of squadron leader – he received an Air Force Cross for his service with this unit. Jerry Pentland retired to Bayview, New South Wales, where he died in November 1983.

Capt Leslie Norman Hollinghurst, from Middlesex, was born on 2 January 1895, and he initially saw service with the Royal Engineers at the start of the war. Commissioned into the 3rd Battalion of the Middlesex Regiment, he too participated in the Gallipoli landings, and then fought in Salonika. Hollinghurst learnt to fly in Egypt, and once back in England he became a delivery and test pilot for a while, prior to going to the reforming No 87 Sqn. 'Holly' survived all the battles of 1918 to become a flight commander, and he eventually received the DFC. He achieved 12 combat victories, sharing the first with his flight commander, Jerry Pentland, on 7 May. He became an ace on 9 August, downing a Pfalz scout and an LVG two-seater.

On the wall of my den I have a water colour of Hollinghurst downing his sixth victory, a Hannover CL, on 3 September – this painting was amongst a series of artworks created by one of his pilots in India post-war. After the Armistice he served with No 79 Sqn in Germany, and this was the first step to a high-ranking RAF career which ended with Hollinghurst becoming an Air Chief Marshal GBE KCB DFC. He saw service in India, where he commanded No 20 Sqn in the early 1930s, and in World War 2 rose to command 38 Group, with the British Airborne Forces. Hollinghurst actually flew operations on D-Day, as well as on the Arnhem landings in September 1944. He died in June 1971.

I got know 'Holly' quite well, for he lived near to me at the top of Putney Hill in the last years of his life, and we had several conversations about his flying in World War 1. He once told me;

'The Dolphin was a splendid aircraft, being both big and lively. We soon discarded the two upward firing Lewis guns, although some pilots did retain just one, especially during the period when we were operating against high flying German two-seater reconnaissance aircraft. We could reach great heights, so for a while our task was to stop these German incursions over our side of the lines. We did this without the slightest worry about oxygen. Pilots today would never dream of going so high without it. I think the idea was that if we couldn't actually get above the Rumplers, a pilot might at least get near enough while still below to fire the Lewis up at them. If we didn't hit them, we might at least drive them east. At this stage of the war the German reconnaissance crews were very nervous about flying over the Allied side.

'The Dolphin was easy to fly, and was strong and manoeuvrable. The pilot had an excellent view and, in my opinion, it was one of the best war machines built. Unfortunately, it stalled rather quickly, and that, and the

No 87 Sqn's Capt L N Hollinghurst DFC, who claimed 12 victories flying the Dolphin. He served with 'B Flight', hence the small white circle painted in the centre of the fighter's wheel cover

'Holly' Hollinghurst is seen posing by the cockpit of his Dolphin, C4167. He flew this machine to France on 27 April 1918, and used it on 6 May when he and another pilot were credited with sending a German two-seater down out of control. C4167 was wrecked in a landing accident just nine days later. The other pilot in this photo is future six-kill ace Lt R A Hewat

peculiar shape of the nose, which prevented the inexperienced pilot from keeping it on the horizon, increased pupils' dislike (of it).'

In September 1924, ex-Capt L N Hollinghurst DFC was a flight lieutenant in the peacetime RAF, attending No 3 Course at the air force Staff College in Andover, in Hampshire. All former airmen who attended these post-war staff college courses had to write of their war experiences, and Leslie Hollinghurst recorded, in part, the following recollections of his time as a Dolphin pilot on the Western Front;

'(My) training squadron at Hounslow was ordered to prepare for France as a Dolphin squadron. It was to have left England early in March 1918, and was completely equipped and awaiting orders to move when the German Offensive began. As a result we had to fly our machines to No 1 Aircraft Supply Depot at St Omer for issue to other squadrons. Considerable care and "tuning-up" had been lavished on our machines, and both pilots and mechanics were very disappointed at having to part with them.

'Having re-equipped with machines, the squadron left for France in April, and was, I think, one of the few units to arrive with no casualties on the way. Enemy aircraft were at this time very quiet in the Nieuport Sector – they had had a rough handling from the Allied squadrons, and did not venture over our side of the line. As a result, all our patrols were carried out over enemy territory, giving the German AA batteries plenty of practice.

'Owing to the "Hun-like" appearance of the Dolphin, our first few patrols created some alarm and consternation amongst the Belgian airmen. After a fight between a Dolphin and some Breguéts, mutual visits between 87 (Sqn) and the Belgian squadrons were necessary to clear the air. Early in June the squadron moved down to a temporary landing ground on the Abbeville-Hesdin road, and joined the 13th Wing, 3rd Brigade.

'About this time (June 1918) considerable difficulty was being found in intercepting the German reconnaissance and photographic machines in the Arras-Albert front. These machines would cross the lines at

Dolphin C8043 'Y' of No 79 Sqn is seen in Germany in 1919. This well-photographed machine was often flown by 'Holly' Hollinghurst during his time as a flight commander with the unit at Bickendorf. He described this particular aircraft as the best Dolphin he ever flew

between 18,000 and 21,000 ft, and were very fast at these altitudes. They were usually able to take their photos and re-cross the lines before our machines could climb up to intercept them, and at such altitudes AA fire was useless.

'On account of the high ceiling of the Dolphin, 87 was employed on interception duty whenever it was important to prevent hostile reconnaissance of our back areas. These line patrols were continuous between dawn and darkness, and allowing for unserviceable machines, it was found that the maximum number which could be kept in the air throughout the day was three.

'At this time considerable trouble was being experienced with the 200-hp Hispano engine. Despite stringent precautions to prevent dust getting into the oil, numerous instances of gear failure occurred owing to the oil feed to the gear becoming blocked – the engine was too lightly built to stand the strain of active service.

'During the summer of 1918 the squadron was engaged in the normal duties of a fighter unit – usually offensive patrols. Formations usually consisted of three sub-formations, each of three or five machines, of one flight apiece. However, a shortage of machines due to engine trouble often rendered composite formations necessary.

'Beyond taking advantage of surprise by every method possible, we developed no definite tactics in aerial fighting. Attempts were made to maintain formation throughout the fight but these were usually unsuccessful, sub-formations became dispersed and a "dogfight" ensued. Unless every pilot in the formation or sub-formation resolutely keeps his place, even to the length of sitting tight and allowing himself to be shot down while his leader, whom he is following, is earning glory by shooting down some other machine, I do not consider that formation will be maintained by single-seaters in a really big fight.

'Although the "herd instinct" impels pilots to keep in formation while on patrol, when a fight commences the enthusiasm and offensive spirit of some will cause them to break away to take advantage of favourable opening for attack, while self-preservation will cause others to perform some evolution which takes them out of their station. It is of course essential that formations be maintained during the dive to attack, and again when rallying after the attack.

'The majority of enemy fighting machines encountered during the autumn of 1918 were very highly decorated. This practice was not allowed in the Royal Air Force but has, I think, much to commend it. Most mechanics delight in giving vent to their artistic capabilities with paint and brush – it does no harm, and certainly increases the pride of both pilots and mechanics in their machines.

'I (must refer) to the high morale of the mechanics. It was undoubtedly one of the great factors which contributed to the success of the Air Service. The mechanics would cheerfully work day and night to keep machines serviceable, sometimes under most disheartening circumstances. They had little leave, and none of the excitement of combat to relieve the monotony of their work.

'Decorations were almost non-existent, yet who did more than the mechanics to contribute to his pilot's success? Nevertheless, their keenness, enthusiasm and determination not to "let their pilot down"

Australian Capt H J Larkin DFC CdG was 'A Flight' commander with No 87 Sqn. A successful ace with 11 victories to his credit, Larkin was accused of taking air fighting 'a bit too seriously' by a number of his squadronmates

never faltered, and was an inspiration to all who had the pleasure of serving with them.'

Australian Henry Joseph Larkin claimed one less kill than 'Holly' Hollinghurst whilst serving with No 87 Sqn. Born in Brisbane on 8 October 1894, he was another who had been with the Royal Engineers in Gallipoli and Egypt as a sergeant, before being wounded by a sniper in September 1915 while serving as a signals clerk to two generals. Transferring to the RFC, Larkin received the French CdG flying with No 5 Sqn on RE 8 observation duties.

Converting to single seaters, he was posted in to command No 87 Sqn's 'A Flight' in 1918, which he did with great success. Larkin was known for his cool, calculating courage, and he only attacked enemy formations when he felt his flight's position and advantage would bring success. Such tactics led certain 'gentleman fliers' on the squadron to question whether he took it all a bit too seriously. Nevertheless, Larkin claimed 11 victories, mostly in C8163, and received the DFC. Returning home after the war, he managed the Larkin Aircraft Supply Company in Melbourne in the 1930s, as well as Australian Aerial Services. Later, Larkin set up business in the Channel Islands after serving with the RAF in World War 2. A noted horticulturist, he died in June 1972.

Henry Arthur Richard Biziou, known as 'Weegee' was born on 18 September 1896. Hailing from Farnborough, in Hampshire, he had been an engineering student prior to volunteering for the RFC. Biziou served as an observer with No 42 Sqn in 1917, and after receiving pilot training he was posted to the newly-formed No 87 Sqn, and flew with it to France in April 1918. He claimed a total of eight victories between May and September – his fourth and fifth coming on 16 September – and he received the DFC and was promoted to captain.

In 1919 Biziou went to the Royal Aircraft Establishment at Farnborough, but was killed in a mid-air collision with a Bristol Fighter on 14 July, aged 22. He is buried in Aldershot.

Capt H A R Biziou DFC became No 87 Sqn's 'B Flight' commander after Pentland was wounded on 25 August. Biziou survived the war with eight victories to his credit, only to be killed in a mid-air collision near Farnborough in July 1919

Joseph Creuss 'Casey' Callaghan was one of three brothers to die whilst flying in World War 1. His younger brother had been killed flying BE 12s with No 19 Sqn in August 1916, whilst his other brother had died in a flying accident in Canada in June 1917, following a period in France with No 5 Sqn. Callaghan himself was 25 when he took command of No 87Sqn.

Born in Dublin in March 1893, he had spent some time in Texas pre-war, but had returned to Ireland in 1914 and joined the 7th Battalion Royal Munster Fusiliers, then the RFC. Callaghan flew FE 2s with No 18 Sqn in 1916, where one of his observers was Sgt B Ankers. As a crew, they were decorated with the

MC and DCM respectively for their bombing and fighting work, having downed a Fokker Eindecker in April 1916.

Callaghan became an instuctor at No 2 School of Aerial Gunnery at Turnberry in 1917, before being given command of No 87 Sqn. He lead from the front in France, claiming four combat victories to become an ace. On 2 July he single-handedly attacked a large formation of Fokker D VIIs, but the leader of the formation, Leutnant Franz Büchner, who was also the commander of *Jasta* 13, shot him down. Büchner ended the war with 40 victories, Callaghan being victory number seven.

Born on 20 February 1897, Charles Edward Worthington came from Leicester. Pre-war, he had received part of his education at Heidelberg College, in Germany, and spoke fluent German. A law student, Worthington joined the Artist's Rifles OTC as a private (then lance corporal) in December 1915, prior to joining the RFC in September 1916. Upon learning to fly, he served with a number of reserve and training units prior to going to No 87 Sqn just before his 21st birthday. Worthington was a stalwart of the unit, scoring evenly during the last year of the war, and often acting as deputy flight commander. His fifth, and final, claim came on 4 October, when he shared in the destruction of a Fokker D VII with his flight commander, Capt Hollinghurst. 'Worthy' left the service in April 1919 and disappeared into obscurity.

Charles John Wharton Darwin from Durham, was 24 and a graduate of the Royal Military College at Sandhurst. He was also a descendant of

Maj J C Callaghan MC was CO of No 87 Sqn from February 1918 until his death in action on 2 July. He became an ace flying the Dolphin, adding four claims to one he had previously made flying an FE 2 with No 18 Sqn in April 1916. Callaghan was shot down by Leutnant Franz Büchner of *Jasta* 13, the Irishman being his seventh of an eventual 40 victims

Lt C E 'Worthy' Worthington and his groundcrew pose with their machine, *"Muddles"*. Serving with No 87 Sqn, Worthington flew across to France with the unit in April 1918 and was still assigned to it when the Armistice came into effect. By then he had claimed five kills

This close-up of Lt Worthington's *"Muddles"* reveals the pilot's seat harness, as well as the Aldis gun sight

Capt C J W Darwin DSO led No 87 Sqn's 'C Flight' in early 1918, before assuming command of the unit in July following the loss of Maj Callaghan. He had scored five victories by war's end

the famous Charles Darwin. His father was also named Charles, and had retired from the Durham Light Infantry as a colonel in 1894 to become a landowner. Educated at Winchester between 1908-11, then in Edinburgh, 'Johnny' Darwin graduated from Sandhurst in 1912.

He served in France with the 2nd Battalion of the Coldstream Guards in 1914-16, although in 1915 he was seconded to the 1st Guards Brigade as a machine-gun officer. In November Darwin was wounded in the right leg, and after recovering, he transferred to the RFC. Joining No 27 Sqn as a pilot in 1917, he flew Martinsyde G 100 Elephants, and later became an instructor at the Central Flying School at Upavon. Darwin was made the flight commander of 'C Flight' in No 87 Sqn prior to it going to France.

He had scored two victories by the time his CO (Callaghan) was shot down and killed on 2 July, and he was then promoted to take his place. Darwin added three more victories to his score to make him an ace, and for his work and leadership, he received the DSO. Granted a permanent commission after the war, Darwin held various posts at the Central Flying School and at RAF Cranwell, before retiring in 1928. He became London Manager for the Bristol Aeroplane Company until World War 2, when he rejoined the RAF as a squadron leader, but he died suddenly on 26 December 1941. His son Christopher was also a fighter pilot with No 87 Sqn in France in 1939-40, but he was later killed in action over North Africa on 7 August 1942.

Richard Alexander Hewat came from Canada, and although he was actually born in North Adams, Massachusetts, on 3 May 1896, he gave his nationality as British. His father was a woollen manufacturer, and Richard was educated at Exeter Academy, Massachusetts, and at a technical college in Huddersfield, England. Hewat joined the RFC in early 1917, having

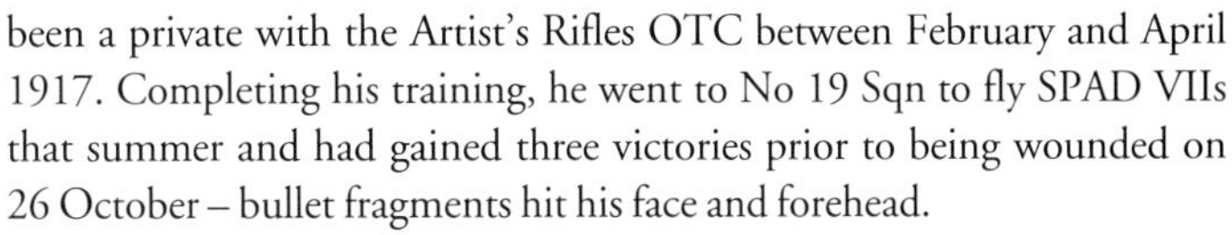

been a private with the Artist's Rifles OTC between February and April 1917. Completing his training, he went to No 19 Sqn to fly SPAD VIIs that summer and had gained three victories prior to being wounded on 26 October – bullet fragments hit his face and forehead.

Upon his recovery towards the end of that year, Hewat (still with a bandaged head) was sent to the new No 87 Sqn, and flying Dolphins, he became an ace on 19 July 1918. 'Dick' gained a third kill with the Sopwith fighter on 9 August, which brought his tally to six. However, five days later he was killed in action by Leutnant Hermann Leptien of *Jasta* 63, becoming the German's fifth victory in an overall tally of seven.

No 87 Sqn's final ace was Canadian Ross Morrison Macdonald. Born in Winnipeg on 3 January 1889, he attended Winnipeg Public School, St Andrews College in Aurora and then the University of Manitoba, back in Winnipeg. Macdonald enlisted into the 79th Battalion of the Cameron Highlanders of Canada at university, and was commissioned in September 1916. Coming to England, he was seconded to the RFC in January 1917, and served as an observer in No 15 Sqn, performing artillery observation sorties, and being mentioned several times in RFC communiqués. He also flew a couple of times with future VC winner, and fellow Canadian, Billy Barker.

After training to be a pilot, 'Mac' was assigned to No 87 Sqn, and he flew with the unit to France in April 1918. Although a little older than most frontline pilots, being 29 when he joined his first fighter squadron, this did not stop Macdonald from claiming five victories during the summer of 1918. Indeed, his run of successes was only stopped when he was shot down near Estourmel and taken prisoner on 29 September. His victories were all scored in C4155, and on his last patrol, at least, it still carried two Vickers and two Lewis guns. There was no obvious claimant for his demise, but *Jasta* 2 were in a fight with F 2bs in the area at the time and claimed three, although only two were lost. Perhaps Macdonald's Dolphin was again confused with a 'Brisfit'. If so, he may have fallen to a *Jasta* Boelcke pilot.

Repatriated after the war, he returned to Canada, and in July 1919 re-joined the Queen's Own Cameron Highlanders. Between the wars Macdonald worked as a manufacturer's agent (a salesman), and during World War 2 he ran his own business. After a lengthy illness, Ross Macdonald died on 29 August 1960, aged 71.

Canadian Lt R A Hewat of No 87 Sqn had claimed three victories in SPAD VIIs with No 19 Sqn in 1917 prior to being wounded in the head. He joined the newly-formed No 87 Sqn early the following year, and scored a further three victories with the Dolphin prior to being killed in action on 14 August 1918

Fellow Canadian Lt Ross Macdonald shot down three high flying Rumplers and two Fokker D VIIs (all in C4155) to become an ace

Ross Macdonald's C4155 'Q' before the unit's distinctive horizontal 'S' marking came into being. He was shot down in this machine on 29 September 1918, and spent the rest of the war as a PoW

DOLPHIN MARKINGS

All Sopwith Dolphins used at the front came in standard camouflage and national markings. Squadron identification markings had been used for some time in France, these generally taking the form of white lines, bars or symbols. On 23 December 1917, RFC HQ issued the following markings for the two squadrons who were about to replace their SPADs with Dolphins – No 19 Sqn would utilise a white square and No 23 Sqn a white triangle, both to be located behind the fuselage roundel.

New units that had been nominated for Dolphins would use the following symbols – a white dumbbell behind the roundel for No 79 Sqn, two vertical lines (or bars) one each side of the fuselage roundel for No 87 Sqn, two slanting white lines behind the roundel for No 85 Sqn and one vertical line behind the roundel for No 90 Sqn.

A new list issued by RFC HQ on 22 March 1918 then decreed that No 23 Sqn was to have a white circle, No 79 Sqn a white square, No 19 Sqn a dumb-bell, No 81 Sqn a half-moon shape lying horizontally, No 91 Sqn a white triangle, No 87 Sqn a horizontal 'S', No 85 Sqn a hexagon and No 90 Sqn a long white line from the top of the forward fuselage sloping back and down to almost the tailplane.

As a matter of general interest, this list was slightly amended on 28 October 1918, with No 91 Sqn now adopting the white triangle and No 81 Sqn the hexagon originally carried by No 85 Sqn. The newly-formed No 93 Sqn took over No 81 Sqn's white half-moon.

No 85 Sqn, in the final analysis, was equipped with SE 5As because of the shortage of Dolphins due to the casualties in the March 1918 offensive, while Nos 81, 91 and 93 Sqns failed to get to France before the Armistice was declared.

No 19 Sqn's identification symbol of a white dumb-bell immediately behind the fuselage roundel was followed by an individual letter, which was repeated on the port upper wing close to the cockpit area. In fact the unit had also decorated its French-coloured SPAD VIIs with a dumb-bell in 1917, although the symbol was applied in black.

Early Dolphin serials were originally marked in white on the aircraft's fin, although this was later changed to black on a white rectangle on the fuselage side, close to the tailplane. Being the first unit to fly the Dolphin, No 19 Sqn has made a point of remembering this

Dolphin C4131 was flown by No 79 Sqn's ranking ace (and the leading Dolphin ace of the war), Capt Fred Gillet, who is seen here standing in front of his machine. The fighter's individual letter 'T' is clearly visible, and it appears that this marking has been applied to both sides of the upper wing. Unusually, the plywood area behind the cockpit has been decorated with black and white squares, which one would have thought made an ideal aiming point for a German fighter pilot! Capt F I Lord scored four kills in this machine (*V G Snyder via Jon Guttman*)

A good view of No 19 Sqn's dumb-bell marking, applied here to Dolphin E4735 'B'. The pilots standing alongside the machine are Lts George Roden and William R Binch

fact on its heraldic badge, which is also adorned with the motto 'They Can Because They Think They Can'.

No 79 Sqn's personal identification marking was a small white square (around half the size of the national marking) immediately aft of the fuselage roundel, followed by a letter, some of which were quite plain in design while others were more decorative. Later, some Dolphins carried the letter immediately aft of the roundel, followed by the white identification square. Aircraft serial numbers were generally applied on the rear fuselage, although some photographs show them both here and across the red, white and blue rudder stripes as well.

No 23 Sqn's identification mark was a small white circle (approximately the size equivalent to the two inner circles of the national marking) immediately aft of the fuselage roundel, followed again by a letter, which was repeated on the top fuselage decking. Again, some of these letters were plain, while others were painted in a more heraldic fashion. The letter was also marked on the top port wing, while the white circle adorned the top of the starboard wing.

The Dolphins of No 87 Sqn did not feature a unit marking when they were flown to France in April 1918, but these aircraft were soon decorated with a 'lazy S' insignia on the fuselage side. Individual aircraft

Dolphin C3898 'D' of No 79 Sqn, lasted until 6 July 1918, by which time Lt C L Lindburg had made one claim with it. Note the unit's white square marking aft of the roundel (*via L A Rogers*)

'Razors' Gillet also flew D3584 'V' during his long spell with No 79 Sqn. It is seen here after the war, the Dolphin's wheel covers marked with 'C Flight's' white circle. White paint has also been applied to the cowling exhaust pipes

Lt Henry of No 79 Sqn climbs aboard Dolphin H7244 'S' in Germany in early 1919. Note the elaborate style of lettering applied to this machine

Dolphin E4589 'A' of 79 Sqn was used by 'Razors' Gillet to claim a solitary victory – Capt L S Ladd also claimed two kills with it. On this occasion the aircraft's individual letter has been applied between the unit marking and the cockade

No 23 Sqn's Capt James Pearson DFC poses with his Dolphin 'U'. Note that the letter has been repeated on the fuselage decking, and that the squadron's white circle marking is also present on the upper surface of the starboard wing. Finally, 'C Flight's' white circle marking adorns the wheel covers

Dolphin F7065 'U' served with No 79 Sqn at Bickendorf during its spell with the Army of Occupation in Germany from 20 December 1918 through to 15 July 1919. This aircraft has had its serial applied across the fin and rudder and the rear fuselage

identification was again by letter, marked immediately aft of the fuselage roundel, and repeated on the top starboard wing. Serials could be on both the rear fuselage or the tail fin or rudder.

No 87 Sqn CO, Maj J C Callaghan, chose 'S' as his personal letter, and one wonders if he had any influence on the choice of squadron marking. If indeed he did, it seems highly likely that he suggested turning his 'S' onto its side – perhaps he had worked at a 'Lazy-S' Ranch during the time

No 87 Sqn's 'B Flight' swapped from individual aircraft letters to numbers in mid-1918, as this photograph of Lt C E Worthington with his '5' clearly shows. He is wearing a standard issue fur 'body-warmer'

No 87 Sqn's Lt A J Golding and his D3775. Note that he has added an 'eye' and a 'rattle' to the squadron marking, turning the 'lazy S' into a snake. Post-war, the snake insignia became the basis of the unit's crest. A small repeat serial number can just be made out under a white tape on the tail-fin. This machine also features extra Lewis guns on the lower wings, with the cord for firing these weapons going into a small hole by the wingroot

American pilot Lt D C Mangan, turned '6' (C8109) over in no-man's land on 25 August when he was forced to crash-land it. He had scored two victories in this machine up to this point in the fighter's short career. Note the wires attached to the tail in order to pull the machine back onto its undercarriage, and the 'dolly' in the foreground to wheel it back to the nearby airfield

he spent in Texas pre-war!? That this 'lazy S' also looked like a snake was not lost on the pilots, and at least one individual added an 'eye' at one end and a snake's 'rattle' at the other. Much later, at the time units were designing, or suggesting designs for their heraldic badges, the personnel of No 87 Sqn chose the snake as their their insignia, with the motto 'The Most Powerful Fear Me'.

It also seems that some attempt was made by No 87 Sqn to identify aircraft by flights through the decoration of wheel covers. 'A Flight' seemed to retain khaki drab covers, 'B Flight' white or light grey, with a white circle in the middle, and 'C Flight' white or light grey with a single khaki or black stripe across the middle.

In the meantime, the Camels of No 65 Sqn appear to have been given the two vertical white stripes originally issued to No 87 Sqn, which replaced the earlier single white horizontal bar along the centre of the fuselage sides. Individual aircraft identification was by letter, although in mid-1918 'B Flight' changed these to numbers for a short period.

DOLPHINS OF THE ACES

By the very nature of things, it is rare that a pilot will fly the same aeroplane in combat for any great length of time, even though he might like to keep and use a particular machine for as long as possible, always provided he liked it, and it in turn suited him. Some aircraft bore a charmed life while others were either lost or damaged early on. Wear and tear also dictated the operational life of some fighters.

Nevertheless, some World War 1 pilots did manage to keep individual aircraft for long periods, and the aces amongst them would often score heavily with a particular machine. Some aircraft too, Dolphins among them, could also be flown by a number of successful pilots whilst serving in the frontline.

The following machines naturally reached their own 'ace' status in terms of victories their pilots achieved;

C4159 – this No 87 Sqn aircraft was flown almost exclusively by Capt A W Vigers MC DFC, and with it he claimed 14 victories. By November 1918 it had 288.45 flying hours recorded in its record book – the flying hour figures quoted for these machines relate directly to the engine of the aircraft and not necessarily the airframe. It might be that some of these Dolphins flew more hours, but the flying hours only relate to the last engine installed. C4159 was originally marked with a 'C' and later, as the

Ronald Bannerman's C3879 (of No 79 Sqn) has its upper left wing changed after it had suffered flak damage over German-held territory. The New Zealander scored 14 of his 17 victories in this aircraft

mount of the 'B Flight' commander, a '1', which looked more like an 'I'. It was, at one stage, fitted with a Lewis guns on each lower wing.

C3879 – No 79 Sqn's Capt R B Bannerman DFC claimed 13 of his victories in this Dolphin. At the beginning of November 1918 it had flown 189.45 hours. The fighter was marked with the letter 'Q'.

C3829 – No 19 Sqn's Capt J Leacroft MC scored six victories in this machine between March and May 1918. It was then assigned to Finley McQuiston, who claimed a further seven kills between June and October. By October the fighter had completed 242.37 flying hours. C3829 wore individual letter 'V' and, possibly, 'P'. It also boasted blue wheel covers.

D5236 – on the strength of No 19 Sqn until lost on 27 October whilst being flown by 2Lt W J Nesbitt (killed), who became the 14th victim of *Jasta* 22's Vizefeldwebel K Bohnenkamp. Capt C V Gardner had claimed four victories with it during July and August, and Capt R A Del'Haye got four more in September and October, and finally Lt C M Moore also added three in September and October. D5236 had completed 167 flying hours by the time it was lost.

C4059 – No 79 Sqn's Capt F W Gillet DFC scored ten victories between 28 September and 8 October 1918 in this aircraft, coded 'F'. Ten days later it had flown 185 hours.

C4136 – Capt L N Hollinghurst DFC scored ten of his victories in this machine (coded 'J') whilst serving with No 87 Sqn. It left the unit on 14 October, and later served with 79 Sqn in 1919.

No 79 Sqn's Capt Fred Gillet sits on the decking of C4059 'F'. The RAF's leading Dolphin ace claimed exactly half of his 20 kills in this machine between 28 September and 8 October 1918

C4017 – No 19 Sqn's Maj A D Carter DSO claimed ten of his thirteen Dolphin victories in this machine (coded 'I') between March and May 1918. He then shot down three more in C4132 in May, and flew C4017 again on the 19th when he was in turn shot down by Paul Billik of *Jasta*. It had completed 52. 78 flying hours prior to its loss.

C8163 – the personal machine of No 87 Sqn's Capt H J Larkin DFC, he scored nine of his eleven kills in it between 21 August and 16 September. Coded 'A', C8163 survived to be flown back to England in 1919.

C3899 – seven victories were scored in this Dolphin during its time with No 19 Sqn, Lt N W Hustings claiming five and Lt M S Gregory two, all in July. It crashed at the unit's airfield at Cappelle on 1 September when its engine seized. C3899 had by then flown 171.44 hours.

C4127 – No 79 Sqn's Capt F I Lord DFC scored at least five kills in this machine in September 1918, Capt F S Wilkins having previously gained two with it on 27 June. Engine failure on 29 September meant that C4127 was sent to No 1 ASD after flying 220.55 hours.

C3799 – Capt G B Irving DFC of No 19 Sqn claimed seven victories in this machine (coded 'B') in April, May and June 1918. It had flown 167.25 hours when another pilot ran into two other Dolphins on take off on 1 September, after which it was sent to No 1 ASD for repair.

C3796 – No 19 Sqn's Capt A B Fairclough MC scored three victories with C3796 in April and May 1918. It was then used by Lt A W Blake, who added three more kills by the end of July. C3796 suffered a petrol line breakage on 9 August after completing 136.17 hours.

C4155 – the personal aircraft of Lt R M Macdonald of No 87 Sqn, he used C4155 (coded 'Q') to score all five of his victories before being shot down in it on 29 September 1918. Lt R A Hewat had also claimed a single kill with the aircraft on 9 August, taking its tally to six in total. C4155 had flown 132.10 recorded hours by the time it was lost.

C4131 – Maj N W Noel, CO of No 79 Sqn, scored one kill in this machine (coded 'T') on 20 May, and Capt F I Lord DFC claimed four victories with it in June and Capt J D Canning one on 17 July. C4131 was declared time expired on 29 August, having flown 211.35 hours.

Capt Joe Larkin's C8163 was photographed bogged down in the mud in the autumn of 1918. The Australian ace scored nine of his eleven combat victories in this aircraft. C8163 survived its service with No 87 Sqn and was flown back to the UK in 1919

These Dolphins of No 87 Sqn's 'C Flight' were photographed at Hounslow just prior to the unit's departure for France on 24 April 1918. Aircraft 'Q' is C4155, which Lt R M Macdonald used to score all five of his victories. He was also shot down in this aircraft on 29 September 1918

C4158 – Capt (later Maj) J W Darwin DSO flew this machine (coded 'M') with No 87 Sqn, and he claimed all five of his victories with it. Capt Pentland made it six by sharing in the destruction of a Rumpler with Lt D C Mangan on 14 August. By 21 November C4158's log noted 152.35 hours.

C3818 – Capt J D I Hardman DFC of No 19 Sqn claimed his first five victories in this machine between 9 May and 1 July 1918. By 23 September it had completed 198.40 flying hours, but a broken oil pipe caused it to be sent away for repair.

D3718 – No 87 Sqn's Capt A A N D Pentland MC DFC scored five victories flying this aircraft (coded 'G') before being wounded in it on 25 August.

C3792 – Capt R A Del'Haye of No 19 Sqn downed five aircraft with this machine in June and July 1918. As he went on leave, it was shot down on 17 July by Leutnant Otto Franke of *Jasta* 30 whilst being flown by 2Lt R E White (PoW). Franke himself was subsequently killed in that action. It had completed 141 flying hours prior to its demise.

D5237 – No 19 Sqn's Lt T H Mercer downed two German aircraft in this machine in October, and Capt J D I Hardman claimed three more later that month.

E4493 – flown mostly by Capt H A R Biziou DFC of No 87 Sqn in September, he shot down five Fokker biplanes with it. During an escort mission on 14 October, Lt C A Bryant had his radiator shot through by a German aircraft, and E4493 had to be sent to No 1 ASD for repair. It had flown just 50.50 hours.

E4712 – No 79 Sqn's Capt J H McNeaney DFC used this aircraft to shoot down four aircraft. Lt J Woolley then made it five when he destroyed a two-seater on 26 October. E4712 suffered from engine over-heating shortly after the Armistice, and it was removed from the squadron after flying 85.55 hours.

E4713 – Lt L H Ray claimed three aircraft and a balloon whilst flying this machine (coded 'R') with No 19 Sqn in September. Lt R C Davies then made it five kills on 30 October when he downed a Fokker D VII over Mons.

SNIPE ACES

The Sopwith 7F.1 Snipe which followed the Dolphin in terms of operational lineage looked every bit the bigger brother of the Sopwith Camel. It was designed from specifications given by the Air Board in early 1917, which called for a single-seat fighter with a speed of 135 mph at 15,000 ft, an average rate of climb of 1000 ft per minute above 10,000 ft, and with an operational ceiling of at least 25,000 ft. It also needed a flying duration of three hours.

The Camel was already at an advanced stage of design when these specifications were issued, and it would be operational in the summer of 1917. A quick glance at the Snipe in the early days needed a second glance to check that it wasn't a Camel – although as we shall read later in this chapter, one No 43 Sqn pilot thought that the Germans sometimes confused the Snipe with a two-seater! However, the Snipe had a slightly larger wing-span than the Camel, 30 ft as opposed to 28 ft, and a length of 19 ft two inches compared with the Camel's 19 ft nine inches, Finally, at nine feet six inches it was a whole foot taller than the Camel.

The Snipe's endurance, however, was little more than the Camel's average of two-and-a-half hours. The new fighter did, however, have a larger engine, being powered by a 230-hp Bentley, rather than the Camel's 140-hp Clerget, 150-hp Gnôme Monosoupape or 150-hp Bentley.

By the time Snipes started coming off the production line in the summer of 1918, the prototypes had had a whole host of niggling technical problems rectified by Sopwith. A specimen was evaluated at No 1 Aeroplane Supply Depot (No 1 ASD) in France in March 1918, and by operational pilots flying with Nos 43 and 65 Sqns. They found favour with the new fighter, although they did not care too much for its

No 43 Sqn Snipe E8001 'D', with Lts Mulcair and Gieger posing for the camera (*via M O'Connor*)

This No 43 Sqn Snipe (E8006) wears a stylised 'C' as its individual aircraft letter. This has not been repeated on the top wing, although the squadron marking (white angled bars) has. The serial is just visible in small white characters/numerals on the stabiliser just ahead of the two white rectangles (*Bruce/Leslie collection*)

This nosed over Snipe provides a good view of the unit markings that were typically applied to most No 43 Sqn aircraft in France in 1918-19 (*via L A Rogers*)

inadequate rudder and heavy ailerons. Once these items had been improved upon, the Snipe began to be built in numbers.

One of the pilots testing the Snipe at No 1 ASD was Lt L N Hollinghurst, a Camel test pilot and future Dolphin ace already referred to in Chapter 2. He took an example up to 24,000 ft in 45 minutes. Lt-Col H A Van Ryneveld MC also flew the new fighter, and noted that it was 'vastly superior to any scout at the front'.

In the event, only three squadrons were destined to receive the Snipe before the Armistice. First was No 43 Sqn, followed by No 4 Sqn of the Australian Flying Corps (AFC) and then No 208 Sqn, although the latter received its examples too late to actually see any action with them.

No 43 Sqn began changing its Camels for Snipes in August 1918, No 4 AFC followed suit in October and No 208 Sqn converted in November.

Apart from these units, two Snipes were sent to No 45 Sqn in late 1918 following the unit's return from the Italian Front. Their planned role was as escort to Independent Force bombers raiding Germany, but the war ended before more examples could reach the unit. These two machines boasted a larger fuel tank, which gave the aircraft an endurance of over four hours. Such a range was crucial when being ordered to escort bombers on long-distance raids. A single modified Snipe was also attached to No 201 Sqn, and its frontline career will be described later.

Equipped with early production machines, No 4 Sqn AFC, and presumably 43 Sqn too, initially suffered with problems caused by the Snipe's machine gun interrupter gear. Indeed, during October, the groundcrews spent most of their time attempting to get the aircraft's 'C-Gears' into a serviceable condition.

On every machine that arrived from the Depot, the pipe lines had to be taken out, annealed to prevent breaking where they were bending, and re-soldered where the lines joined the trigger motors, generators and reservoir. Most pipe lines arrived soft-soldered at these joints, and they did not stand up to the constant vibrations, quickly breaking away. Every pipe had to be examined, and in some cases it was even found that brass filings from manufacture had blocked them. Washers had also been fitted badly, or the wrong way round, and damping valve springs omitted. In addition, every gun needed the connecting rod lengthened – an average of .013 of an inch for each gun.

As well as these problems, it was discovered that most of the Aldis gun sights had been mounted too low for the average pilot, which meant new windscreens so that new cut-outs could be made in order to raise the sights to a better level!

Another problem with the new machine was that inspection doors had to be made in the side of the cowling to allow the ammunition bins to be examined prior to flight to check that they carried the required amount, and for convenience of fitting the belted gun ammunition without taking off the cowling every time the magazines were reloaded. All this took time, and further delayed the Snipe from making its combat debut against the enemy.

The pilots of No 43 Sqn pose for an official photograph at Cologne in December 1918. They are, from left to right, at the rear, G Todd, W H Temple, W H Statham, G H Smith, W G Holder, D J Stewart, E C Robinson, W B Giles and E G Weaver. Middle, Brodie, Thornhill, R L Houlding, J H Johnson, J G Murray, C A Mitchell, G F Geiger, G R Howsam and E Mulcair. And front, G W Shuter, Capt A H Orlebar, Maj C C Miles, Capt C C Banks and J S Swales (*Bruce/Leslie collection*)

No 43 Sqn's Capt C F King sits in the cockpit of his near-new Snipe. Note his initials *CK* painted on the fighter's fuselage immediately beneath him (*via M O'Connor*)

No 43 Sqn

No 43 Sqn was a well-established fighter unit which had been formed in early 1916. After operating a variety of aircraft, it finally went to France equipped with the Sopwith 1 1/2 Strutter two-seat fighter-reconnaissance aircraft in January 1917. After eight months of long-range reconnaissance missions, and many air battles, it changed to single-seat Camels in September 1917 – at the same time it lost its observers. The unit continued to serve in the forefront of the action on the Western Front for the next year, producing a number of well known aces (which will be covered in The *Camel Aces* book planned for publication in this series in 2003).

By the time the Sopwith Snipe began to arrive at No 43 Sqn's Fienvillers base, south-west of Doullens, in August 1918, its commanding officer was Maj C C Miles MC – the unit later moved to Senlis-le-Sec, north-east of Paris. The pilots continued to fly the Camel until mid-September 1918 due to the Snipe being restricted from flying over enemy territory. This dictate was relaxed by the time the whole unit had been re-equipped, and the first Snipe claim came on 27 September.

Between then and the end of the war, No 43 Sqn claimed just 11 victories – two destroyed and nine out of control. All but one of these victories were over Fokker D VIIs,

Capt C F King MC DFC CdeG claimed 22 victories with No 43 Sqn, the last three being scored with the Snipe

Snipe E8015 'E' was routinely flown by Lt E Mulcair (seen here), who gained two victories with it. Immediately behind the fighter is Snipe 'F' E8013. While 'E' has its letter and the two bars repeated on the top wing, 'F' does not

the eleventh kill being a Hannover CL two-seater. Most of these claims were made during escort missions (primarily for DH 9s of No 107 Sqn), which the squadron undertook in the final weeks of war.

That first victory was shared by two aces, Capt C F King and Lt C C Banks. Cecil Frederick King was born in Sevenoaks, Kent, on 19 February 1899, although he was living in Chelmsford when he joined the colours. He had been educated at Charterhouse School, where he had joined the OTC in 1912. King suffered a broken arm in April 1915, which delayed both his training and education, but in February 1917 he transferred to the RFC from the Essex Regiment, and was commissioned in May.

No 43 Sqn's Capt C C Banks MC DFC claimed the final three of his dozen kills with the Snipe

Joining No 43 Sqn in late 1917, King had won the MC by early 1918, and had been given command of 'B Flight' during March of that year. He later added the French CdG and the DFC to his MC. King's tally of victories by early August totalled 19, and he added three more flying Snipe E8031 in the last weeks of the war.

Cecil King's last combat report, dated early afternoon of 30 September 1918 above Aulnoye, reads;

'I attacked, with the rest of my flight, six Fokker biplanes from underneath as they were preparing to attack us. After about two minutes scrapping at close quarters,

The pilots and mechanics of 'A Flight', No 43 Sqn, pose for the camera in the final weeks of the war. The pilots, all sat in the front row, are, front left to right, Lts E Mulcair (two victories), E G Weaver and J S Swales, Capt C C Banks, and Lts G R Howsam, G F Geiger and C A Mitchell

Canadian ace Capt G R Howsam MC (centre) scored his 13th, and final, victory flying Snipe E8013 on 30 October 1918 – this was also No 43 Sqn's last successful aerial engagement of the war. Note Howsam's long-barrelled Luger tucked into the belt of his coat

I got in a very good burst directly behind one, which went down in a slow spin. Lt Mulcair confirmed having seen this machine spin right down out of sight. Shortly after this my oxygen cylinder was blown up, warping my aeroplane, and making it unsafe, so I had to return home.'

Having survived the Great War, King was tragically killed in a flying accident on 24 January 1919 when his Snipe collided with an identical machine from the newly-equipped No 70 Sqn over Cologne. He was still a month short of celebrating his 20th birthday.

As previously mentioned, Capt King had shared the Snipe's first victory on 27 September with Lt Charles Chaplin Banks. Hailing from Llundudno, in North Wales, the latter individual had been a schoolmaster pre-war. Initially serving with the 5th Battalion of the Royal Welsh Fusiliers, 'Sandy' Banks joined the RFC in October 1916, and was posted to No 44 Home Defence Sqn after learning to fly. Having initially flown Sopwith 1 1/2 Strutters, the unit re-equipped with Camels in August 1917, and Banks used one of the latter fighters to share in the destruction of a Gotha bomber during a raid on England in January 1918 – he was awarded an MC for this action, having been Mentioned in Despatches the previous month.

Joining No 43 Sqn in France towards the end of February 1918, Banks had scored ten victories on the Camel by August. Transferred as an instructor to No 4 Fighter School for a rest in mid-June, he returned to No 43 Sqn in September, and added three more kills on Snipes (all whilst flying E8028) in very quick succession. Banks was awarded the DFC and received another 'Mention', and ended the war as a captain, leaving the service in January 1919. Following in his father's footsteps, Charles Banks's son saw action in World War 2 as a fighter pilot, being shot down over Italy and taking up arms with the partisans. Later captured by the Germans, he was duly executed.

Another established No 43 Sqn Camel ace to see action with the Snipe was George Robert Howsam, a Canadian from Toronto (he was born in Port Perry, Ontario, on 29 January 1895). Wounded whilst serving with the Canadian army in France, Howsam joined the RFC while on leave back in Canada, receiving his commission on 19 August 1917. Posted to No 70 Sqn, equipped with Camels, in late 1917, he had claimed 12 victories by mid-March 1918 – and been awarded the Military Cross. Wounded on 24 March and then rested, Howsam was sent to No 43 Sqn as a flight commander just after it had converted to Snipes.

On 30 October he shot down a Fokker D VII in flames during the unit's last successful air battle, flying Snipe E8013. This brought his final score to 13. Howsam later served in the RCAF, and in World War 2 was Air Officer Commanding No 4 Training Command. He retired as an Air Vice Marshal CBE in 1946, and from 1950 to 1957 he was Co-ordinator of the Alberta Civil

Snipe E8013 'F' is seen in poor shape after enduring a particularly heavy landing. Note that the fighter's individual letter has been applied to the top port wing, rather than the starboard one as has previously been the case. Capt Howsam claimed his final victory in this machine (*Bruce/Leslie collection*)

Defence Organisation. He died in Victoria, British Columbia, on 16 April 1988.

Another ace to score a Snipe victory was 21-year-old Augustus Henry Orlebar. Hailing from Bedfordshire, he had a long military career which started in the army when he was commissioned into the 1st/15th Bedfordshire Regiment (TF) in January 1915. Wounded by a Turkish sniper in October during the ill-fated Gallipoli campaign, Orlebar returned to England and joined the RFC. Posted to No 19 Sqn in late 1916, he initially flew BE12s – the single-seat fighter version of the BE 2 reconnaissance machine – but his first two victories came whilst flying SPAD VIIs in the Spring of 1917.

Eight-kill ace Capt A H Orlebar (left) is seen with Lts Cooper and Holding. (*via M O'Connor*)

After a rest period, Orlebar went to No 73 Sqn in 1918, where he brought his score to six during the March battles. Wounded for a second time, he had recovered sufficiently by late 1918 to be posted to No 43 Sqn as a flight commander. On 27 and 29 September he drove down Fokker biplanes out of control (in E8021 and E8024), bringing his final score to eight.

Orlebar's combat report for the 29th (an action which took place at 6000 ft over Remaucourt at 1015 hrs) reads;

'I was below the remainder of the formation with Lt Thomas. I saw machines fighting on my level and Bristol Fighters above me. I attacked the enemy aircraft as he crossed me, and he turned away from me. I went on firing as he dived. When I was about 30 yards from him, he turned over on one wing and disappeared. I saw him soon afterwards and he seemed to be going down in a series of stalls. I watched him down to 1000 ft, and was then attacked myself.'

At Staff College after World War 1, Orlebar wrote the following about the Snipe in his War Experiences essay;

'We were chiefly employed on close escort duty with bombing formations of DH 9s. Thus advantages in performance of the best machine on the front were to a great extent lost. Five minutes away from the bombing formation to engage enemy machines meant anything up to forty minutes in rejoining the bombers, even if they were in sight. Thus, if we broke away in order to drive off an enemy attack, the bombers lost their protection for the remainder of the raid, and further, whenever we did engage the enemy, he possessed nearly every tactical advantage.

Right
These Snipes were photographed on Fienvillers airfield in October 1918. Again, a variety of serial locations are visible – 'L' (E8034) has its serial on the tail and fuselage, 'K' in neither place and 'Q' (E8032) only on the fuselage. Note that the squadron marking was not repeated on the top wing (*Bruce/Leslie collection*)

Pilots of No 43 Sqn get together for an informal photograph at Senlis on 10 October 1918. They are, from left to right, rear, J H Forbes, D J Stewart, G M Smith, J P Bernigaud, J W Milner, J G Murray, H F Davison, W H Temple, G Todd and J H Johnson. And front, W B Raynor, H C Hull, Capt A H Orlebar, R L Houlding, Capt C R Keary, Maj C C Miles MC, W B Giles and Capts C F King and C C Banks (*Bruce/Leslie collection*)

This line-up of No 43 Sqn Snipes was seen at Cologne post-war, E8015 'E' being parked second from the right. Note the centre fuselage bomb rack on the Snipe in the foreground (*Bruce/Leslie collection*)

'On the few Offensive Patrols we carried out, some success was indeed obtained, and at first enemy pilots seemed to mistake the Snipe for a two-seater, and attempted to get below us (to avoid the non-existent rear gunner) rather than dive from above.

'A few experimental oxygen sets were issued to us for high flying, and the difference in efficiency on patrols and in fatigue afterwards between pilots who had oxygen and those without it was very marked. The usual height of patrols was about 17,000 ft, and it was nearly always those with oxygen that saw hostile machines first, and engaged them with good effect. I think this emphasises very clearly the need of oxygen for the development of efficiency in high flying.

Another view of E8001, seen on page 71. Lt E Mulcair still looks interested for the camera, but one of the pilots has discovered something of more importance in his newspaper! Note the 'D' and squadron markings on the fighter's top wings (*Bruce/Leslie collection*)

'In September 1918 we took part in the offensive about Cambrai from an aerodrome near Albert, although we occasionally escorted bombing formations to objectives as far north as Audenarde. In order to put the objective within our fuel range, our Snipes refuelled at an aerodrome on the sector closest to the objective, before starting out to rendezvous with the bombers.'

Remaining in the RAF, Orlebar flew with the Aeroplane Experimental Establishment from 1919 to 1925, during which time he gained an Air Force Cross. In 1929 he was a part of the victorious Schneider Trophy Team (gaining a Bar to his AFC), and in 1934 he became Senior Air Staff Officer with the RAF in Aden. During World War 2 Orlebar commanded RAF Northolt. He died of cancer in August 1943.

MARKINGS

No 43 Sqn marked both its Camels and Snipes with two inverted white bars on either side of the fuselage roundel, while an individual letter in white came aft of these markings. The letter was repeated on the upper port wing, inboard of the roundel. At one period the two inverted bars were also depicted on the top wing, one bar being applied on either side of the centre section cut-out.

Serial numbers appeared on the rear fuselage, black letters on a white rectangle, or later in white on the stabiliser. In some photographs a very small serial also appears on the top of the lower portion of the stabiliser.

Capt T C R Baker DFC scored six of his twelve victories in Snipes with No 4 Sqn AFC, but was killed in action one week before the Armistice

No 4 Sqn, Australian Flying Corps

This unit had started life as No 71 Sqn RFC, staffed mostly by Australian volunteers. It began receiving Sopwith Camels in December 1917, and was re-numbered No 4 Sqn AFC the following month. It duly proved to be one of the most aggressive Camel-equipped units in France during the last year of the war, and by the time it began receiving Snipes in October new fighters, its pilots had claimed nearly 200 victories. This form continued with the new Sopwith fighter, No 4 Sqn AFC being credited with a further 35 kills between 26 October and 4 November!

At this time the unit was part of 80 Wing, commanded by Col L A Strange DSO MC, and it usually flew as top cover to other aircraft within the wing – Bristol Fighters, Camels, SE 5s and DH 9s.

The first actual Snipe victory credited to No 4 Sqn AFC was scored on 9 October when 2Lt Thomas Henry Barkell, a former motor mechanic from Sydney, flamed a kite balloon in E8032 at 0955 hrs. This victory made him an ace. His four earlier kills had all come on Camels during September. Barkell gained two more victories on 26 October over Tournai, although he was wounded in the leg during this action.

Born in Randwick, New South Wales, in 1892, Barkall's war service had started in October 1916 when he joined the army, then transferred to the AFC. Assigned to No 3 Sqn AFC as a sergeant until he became a pilot

Capt Baker used E8069 '2' to gain his first Snipe victory on 26 October 1918. This was his seventh kill overall (*via L A Rogers*)

A frontal view of Baker's E8069 '2' (*via L A Rogers*)

in 1918, Barkell was awarded the DFC soon after 'making ace'. After the war he became a commercial pilot.

Aside from Barkall's two kills on 26 October, the unit had also 'bagged' three more victories. Two days later No 4 Sqn AFC enjoyed the first of four big-tally days, with eight victories, followed on the 29th with eleven claims, seven on the 30th and finally three on 4 November. By this date the unit had moved from Serny to Auchel, then, because of the rapid ground advances, to Grand Ennetiéres, near Lille. This constant base shifting effectively curtailed combat time in the air.

Another pilot to enjoy success with the Snipe was Lt Thomas Charles Richmond Baker Military Medal (MM) and Bar from South Australia. Born in Smithfield on 2 May 1897, the former bank clerk had 'made ace' at the start of October 1918 whilst still flying the Camel. He had exactly doubled his tally by the end of the month, with one kill on the 26th, three on the 28th and one each on the 29th and 30th.

Joining the Australian Imperial Forces in July 1915, Baker had served with the 16th Battery, 6th Australian Field Artillery Brigade. He had been awarded his MM for service with the artillery, and then received a Bar to this before transferring to the AFC in September 1917. Having brought his score to 12, Baker was shot down and killed on 4 November 1918in the unit's last big air fight of the war.

The Australians had 'mixed it' with Fokker biplanes from JG III, and they lost five Snipes – four fell to the commander of *Jasta* 2 'Boelcke', Karl Bolle, these being the German's 33rd to 36th kills. Leutnant Ernst Bormann of the same unit got the fifth for his 16th victory. Baker's award of the DFC was gazetted in February 1919. He was buried at Escanaffles, in Belgium.

Lt Arthur John Palliser came from Launceston, Tasmania, having been born on the 'apple isle' on 2 March 1890. Like Barkell, he too had been a motor mechanic pre-war, but with the Australian Army Service Corps. Transferring to the AFC, he joined No 4 Sqn after earning his 'wings', and in the autumn of 1918 he gained two victories flying Camels. Claiming a further five with the Snipe, Palliser was also shot down and killed during the 4 November action with JG III, flying E8064. He was buried at Anvaing, in Belgium.

Capt Elwyn Roy King, known as 'Bo', hailed from Bathurst, New South Wales, where he was born on 13 May 1894. Employed in the motor engineering business when war broke out in Europe, like so many of his countrymen, his first service was with the Australian Light Horse. Once he had transferred to the AFC and become a pilot, King was sent to No 4 Sqn.

His Camel claims totalled 19 between May and early October 1918, and he added a further seven scalps from 28 October as 'A Flight' commander, flying the Snipe – including two during the last big battle of 4 November. All of King's Snipe kills had been over Fokker D VIIs, with the exception of a solitary LVG two-seater that he destroyed on 29 October. His war record brought him both the DSO and DFC.

Returning to Australia, King resumed his engineering career, and during World War 2 he volunteered for service with the Royal Australian Air Force, but died through illness while station commander of RAAF Point Cook in November 1941.

Capt E R 'Bo' King DSO DFC claimed seven kills in Snipe E8050 with No 4 Sqn AFC in the last weeks of the war. These successes boosted his final tally to 26 victories

Lt George Jones DFC claimed three Snipe victories with No 4 Sqn AFC, taking his overall tally to seven by war's end

George Jones, from Rushworth, Victoria, reached his 22nd birthday shortly after the Armistice (22 November). Like several other pilots of note within No 4 Sqn AFC, he had started out as yet another motor mechanic, before joining the Australian Light Horse.

Jones saw active duty in Palestine and Gallipoli with the 9th Sqn, Light Horse, and once back in Egypt he became a corporal with the Camel Corps, before transferring to the AFC. He joined No 1 Sqn AFC as a mechanic, then transferred to No 2 Sqn when it arrived in England in 1917. Trained as a pilot, Jones went to No 71 Sqn, which became No 4 Sqn AFC, in January 1918, having been commissioned two months earlier.

He scored four Camel victories (and collected a wound on 24 March 1918), but became an ace flying the Snipe by downing his fifth and sixth victories on 29 October, adding a seventh on 4 November. Promoted to captain, and awarded a DFC, Jones decided to remain in the service post-war and rose to senior rank, finally becoming Chief of the Air Staff (RAAF). In 1948 he became an Air Marshal KBE (Knighted in March 1954 during a visit to Australia by HM the Queen) CB, and later retired to Melbourne. Jones then worked with the Commonwealth Aircraft Corporation for five years, and served as a director on the board of Ansett Transport Industries for 20 years. At the time of his death in August 1992, he was the last surviving Australian air ace of World War 1, as well as the last Australian Service Chief from World War 2.

Born at Clifton Hill, Victoria, on 18 July 1895, Norman Charles Trescowthick worked for a boot manufacturer in Alphington, Melbourne until he joined the AFC. His first six victories came with the Camel, and he gained one further kill flying Snipe E8064 on 30 October. Trescowthick was awarded the DFC, and became a flight commander.

No 4 Sqn AFC's last big action came on 4 November in the fight with *Jagdgeschwader* Nr.III, and in particular the Fokkers of *Jasta* 2 (Boelcke). To quote from the Official History of the Australians in World War 1;

Snipe E8198 'U' clearly shows the No 4 Sqn AFC marking forward of the roundel, with the fighter's individual letter being repeated on the top starboard wing (*via L A Rogers*)

Snipes from No 4 Sqn AFC's 'B Flight' (*via L A Rogers*)

'King, leading the Snipes, escorted the bombers back across the lines and then, seeing 12 Fokkers following his formation, turned back, climbed, and dived on the enemy's leader. He fired 150 rounds into this machine, which stalled, fell on its side, and dropped earthward on its back. A general scrimmage ensued. King fastened on to another Fokker, which was shooting on the tail of a Snipe, and sent it down in flames after four rapid bursts of fire at 100-ft range. G Jones attacked the rearmost German of the formation, overran it during his opening fusillade, and sped on to another, which was attacking H A Wilkinson. This Fokker also fell in flames. Wilkinson, delivered from it, dropped with a quick turn on two more Fokkers behind and below him, fired a close-range burst into the nearest one and saw it fall out of control.

'Such is the vignette of a short and willing encounter preserved in the laconic narrative of the Australian pilots. The fight lasted but two or three minutes, and died out in the usual way, with machines spread over a wide area and making to regain formation. When the Snipes had re-formed it was found that three splendid pilots had been lost in the action – Baker (a flight commander) and Lts Palliser and P W Symons.'

Markings

No 4 Sqn AFC's identification mark was one small vertical white bar, applied forward of the fuselage roundel. It was wider than other RAF bars, and not overly long – it did not extend beyond the diameter of the cockade. Individual aircraft marking was by a white letter aft of the cockade, repeated on the top starboard wing for 'A' and 'C Flights'. 'A Flight' used letters A to G and 'C Flight' S to Z. The wing letter was positioned outboard of the centre section, and extended almost the full chord of the wing. 'B Flight' used numbers 1 to 8. The three flights also had different coloured wheel covers, 'C Flight's' being white.

Canadian 50-kill ace Capt W G 'Billy' Barker VC DSO and Bar MC and two Bars (*Bruce/Leslie collection*)

VC Action

One cannot conclude reference to the Sopwith Snipe's brief service in World War 1 without mentioning the last aerial battle fought by Canadian ace William George Barker DSO MC, for which he received the Victoria Cross.

'Billy' Barker was born on 3 November 1894 in Dauphin, Manitoba. As a young man he became an accomplished horseman, and an excellent shot with a rifle. Just prior to the start of World War 1, Barker was living in Winnipeg, and in November 1914 he enlisted in the 1st Battalion of the Canadian Mounted Rifles as a private. By the time he arrived in France, via England, Barker had already applied to join the RFC, and he flew as an observer with No 9 Sqn (BE 2s). He later served with Nos 4 and 15 Sqns, but then trained as a pilot and returned to No 15 Sqn in early 1917.

Whilst flying two-seaters Barker won the MC and Bar, and having tasted air combat, he asked for transfer to single-seat fighters and was sent to No 28 Sqn, which was equipped with Camels. Not long after he began flying with this unit in France, it was sent to the Italian Front, and during 1918 Barker's score of combat successes rose so that by the end of the summer he had amassed 42 victories – 37 aircraft and nine balloons. This success had resulted in the DSO and Bar, as well as the Italian Silver Medal for Military Valour, being added to his name.

Returning to England in September 1918, Barker could have easily sat out the war as an instructor, but he persuaded the 'powers' to let him return to France in order to gain up-to-date knowledge of air fighting on the Western Front in order to impart them to his pupils. He was attached to No 201 Sqn, which had Camels, but he took with him a Sopwith Snipe E8102 to evaluate its capability.

His period of attachment to No 201 Sqn was for two weeks, but during that time combat eluded him, and on 27 October he had to return to England. Taking off, he flew close to the lines on his way home – for a last look – and found a German two-seater which he attacked and shot down. The observer was killed, and as the machine fell earthwards, breaking up as it did so, the pilot took to his parachute. Barker was so focused on his kill, and particularly the parachuting airman, that he failed to see a flight of Fokker D VIIs diving down on him.

Sopwith Snipe E8102 in which Capt W Barker DSO MC won his Victoria Cross in a single-handed action on 27 October 1918. Note the crushed tail-fin and engine cowling. The white bar markings are similar to those used by Barker to decorate his Camel in Italy earlier in the year

Over the next several minutes he fought like a demon against a number of Fokkers, being severely wounded in the right thigh, then having his left elbow shattered and finally being hit in the left thigh. With each wound he fainted momentarily, and each time he came round he found the air seemingly full of German fighters. With smoke pouring from his engine, Barker even sought to ram any fighters that came into view. He was finally forced down to make a crash-landing just behind the British lines, breaking his nose in the process.

Despite this engagement being seen, and reported on, from the ground, it has never been conclusively discovered who Barker had been fighting. His report, added to statements from those on the ground, appear to suggest he had shot down three Fokker biplanes, bringing his overall score to 50. However, it is difficult to identify which German unit had engaged him, and the loss of three Fokkers seems excessive despite the sparcity of records at this late stage of the war.

Barker did not write the combat report of this action – he was too badly injured – so it is unclear who provided the squadron CO (Maj C M Leman) with all the information. Whatever had occurred, Barker received the Victoria Cross for this action, in which the number of Fokkers fluctuates between 15 and 60. Later, Barker was always reticent to speak of this air fight, some say because of his modesty, or perhaps he was mindful that he had made a mistake and been caught napping. That he himself felt he had not deserved the acclaim is another matter. He would always talk of his more – to him – heroic escapades in Italy.

The citation for Barker's Victoria Cross reads:

'On the morning of the 27th October 1918, this officer observed an enemy two-seater over the Forét de Mormal. He attacked this machine, and after a short burst it broke up in the air. At the same time a Fokker biplane attacked him and he was wounded in the right thigh, but managed despite this to shoot down the enemy aeroplane in flames.

'He then found himself in the middle of a large formation of Fokkers, who attacked him from all directions, and was again wounded in the left thigh, but succeeded in driving down two of the enemy in a spin.

'He lost consciousness after this and his machine fell out of control. On recovery he found himself being again attacked heavily by a large formation, and singling out one machine, he deliberately charged and drove it down in flames.

'During this fight his left elbow was shattered and he again fainted, and on regaining consciousness he found himself still being attacked, but, notwithstanding that he was now severely wounded in both legs and his left arm shattered, he dived on the nearest machine and shot it down in flames.

'Being greatly exhausted, he dived out of the fight to regain our lines, but was met by another formation, which attacked and endeavoured to cut him off, but after a hard fight he succeeded in breaking up this formation and reached out lines, where he crashed on landing.

'This combat, in which Maj Barker destroyed four enemy machines (three of them in flames) brought his total successes up to 50 enemy aeroplanes destroyed, and is a notable example of the exceptional bravery and disregard of danger which this very gallant officer has always displayed throughout his distinguished career.

View of the starboard side of Barker's Snipe. The main section of the fuselage of this machine is a prized exhibit in the Canadian War Museum in Ottawa (*Bruce/Leslie collection*)

'Maj Barker was awarded the Military Cross on 10th January 1917, first Bar on 18th July 1917, Distinguished Service Cross on 18th February 1918, second Bar to Military Cross on 16 September 1918, and Bar to Distinguished Service Order on 2nd November 1918.'

Barker survived his injuries and went into aviation in his native Canada, also serving in the embryo Canadian Air Force between 1920-24, then started a tobacco business. In early 1930 he became vice-president of the Fairchild Aviation Corporation of Canada, but was killed in a flying accident in a Fairchild KR-21 (CF-AKR) on 12 March that same year at Rockcliffe aerodrome, Ottawa.

As a matter of interest, South African ace Capt A F W B Proctor VC DSO MC and Bar DFC, who had gained 54 victories flying SE 5s with No 84 Sqn, was killed in a Snipe crash. On 21 July 1921 he was practising aerobatics in E8220 whilst training for that year's Hendon Air Pageant. Attempting a slow roll off the top of a loop, he appeared to lose control, went into a spin and crashed at Enford, in Wiltshire, about a mile from the airfield.

MARKINGS

'Billy' Barker's Sopwith Snipe had standard camouflage and five large white stripes on the rear fuselage, aft of the roundel. They went right over the fuselage but did not extend to the underside – note that this was not No 201 Sqn's identifying marks. When Barker had served with No 139 Sqn in Italy, his personal Camel had carried four white bands (later seven) in the same location.

This Camel also boasted a tiny flat metal red devil, thumbing its nose, as a foresight on the right-hand machine gun. This Barker had retained upon returning to England, and he used it on the right-hand gun of the Snipe. While crunched and damaged, E8102 was not destroyed, and several photographs of it show minimum damage – a crumpled tail fin and slightly crumpled top leading edge, both denoting the machine had turned over, as well as a broken undercarriage. The main section of the fuselage is a prized exhibit in the Canadian War Museum in Ottawa.

APPENDICES

Appendix 1

Sopwith Dolphin Aces

Name	Nationality	Unit	Aircraft Destroyed	OOC Kite Balloons	Dolphin Total	Overall War Total
Capt F W Gillet	US	79	17	3	20	20
Capt R B Bannerman	NZ	79	16	1	17	17
Capt A W Vigers	Br	87	6	8	14	14
Capt A A N D Pentland	Aust	87	7	6	13	23
Maj A D Carter	Can	19	8	5	13	29
Capt L N Hollinghurst	Br	87	8	4	12	12
Capt G B Irving	Can	19	3	9	12	12
Capt F I Lord	US	79	8	3	12	12
Capt J W Pearson	US	23	6	6	12	12
Capt H J Larkin	Aust	87	5	6	11	11
Capt A B Fairclough	Can	19/23	7	3	10	19
Capt C V Gardner	Br	19	6	4	10	10
Capt F McQuiston	Br	19	3	7	10	10
Capt R A Del'Haye	Br	19	4	5	9	9
Capt J D I Hardman	Br	19	4	5	9	9
Capt H A R Biziou	Br	87	7	1	8	8
Capt J Leacroft	Br	19	5	3	8	22
Lt N W Hustings	Br	19	2	5	7	7
Lt H A White	US	23	3	4	7	7
Lt L H Ray	Br	19	2	4	6	7
Capt J DePencier	Can	19	1	5	6	8
Lt T A Aldridge	Br	19	1	4	5	5
Lt A W Blake	SA	19	2	3	5	5
Lt H N Compton	Can	23	4	1	5	5
Maj C J W Darwin	Br	87	4	1	5	5
Lt R M Macdonald	Can	87	2	3	5	5
Lt C E Worthington	Br	87	4	1	5	5
Capt J H McNeaney	Br	79	5	0	5	5
Lt E Taylor	US	79	1	4	5	5

Pilots who became aces, or added to their score, whilst flying the Dolphin

Name	Nationality	Unit	Aircraft Destroyed	OOC Kite Balloons	Dolphin Total	Overall War Total
Maj J C Callaghan	Irish	87	2	2	4	5
Capt P Huskinson	Br	19	2	2	4	11
Lt R A Hewat	Can	87	2	1	3	6
Lt H A F Goodison	Br	23	2	1	3	5
Capt E Olivier	Br	19	2	0	2	8
Capt W M Fry	Br	79	1	0	1	11
Capt L M Mansbridge	Br	23	0	1	1	5

APPENDIX 2

Awards to Dolphin Pilots

Distinguished Service Order	Maj C J W Darwin
Bar to Distinguished Service Order	Maj A D Carter DSO
Military Cross	Capt A B Fairclough
Bar to Military Cross	Capt P Huskinson MC Capt J Leacroft MC
Distinguished Flying Cross	Maj A R Arnold DSC Capt R B Bannerman Capt H A R Biziou Capt R A Del'Haye Capt C V Gardner Capt F W Gillet Capt J D I Hardman Capt L N Hollinghurst Capt G B Irving Capt H J Larkin CdG Capt F I Lord Lt J H McNeaney Capt F McQuiston Capt J W Pearson Capt A A N D Pentland MC Capt H V Puckridge Lt F J Stevenson Capt A W Vigers MC Lt F Woolley Lt H A White.
Bar to Distinguished Flying Cross	Capt R B Bannerman DFC Capt F W Gillet DFC
Belgian *Croix de Guerre*	Lt J A Aldridge
Michael the Brave, 3rd class (Romania)	Lt L H Ray

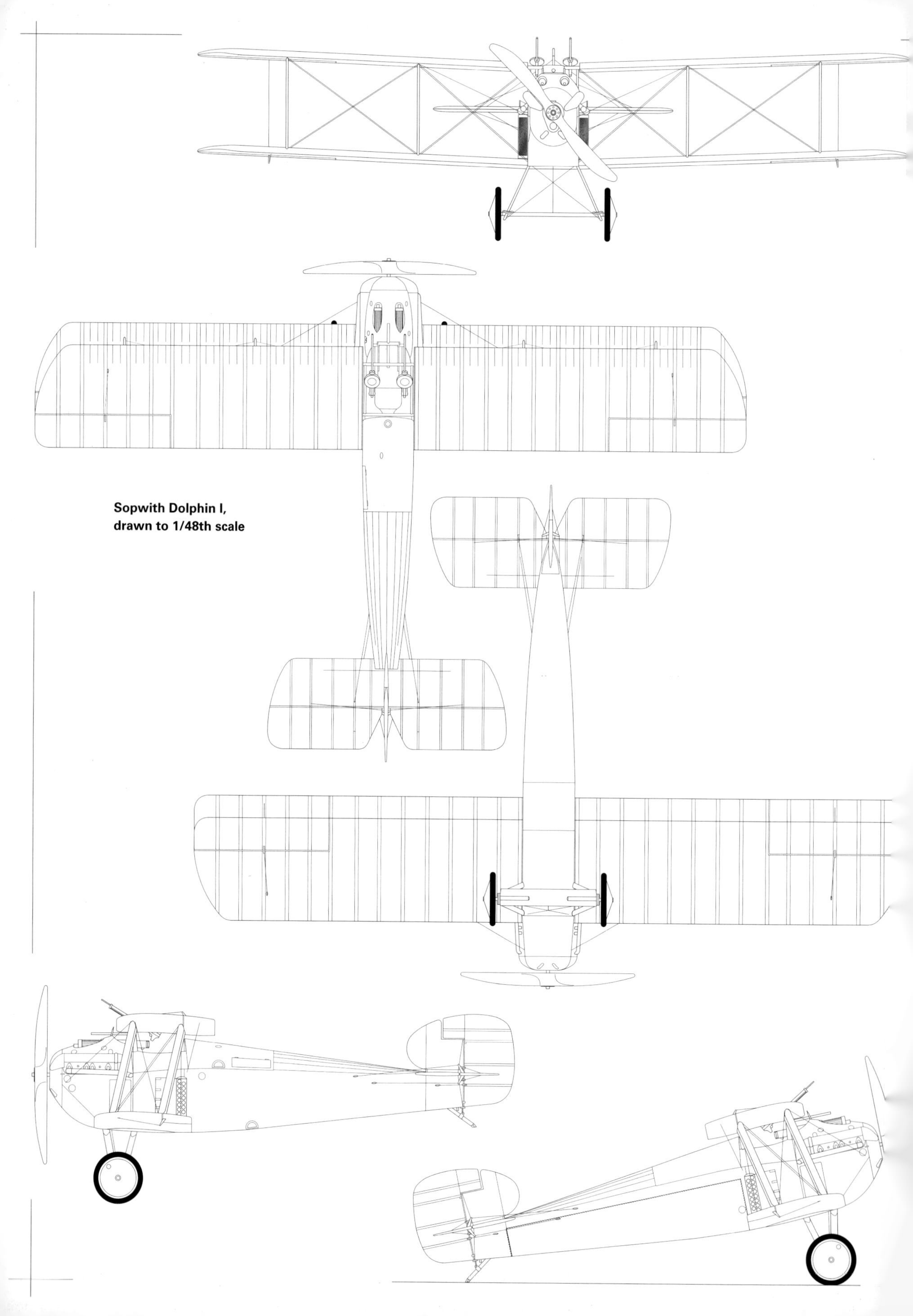

Sopwith Dolphin I, drawn to 1/48th scale

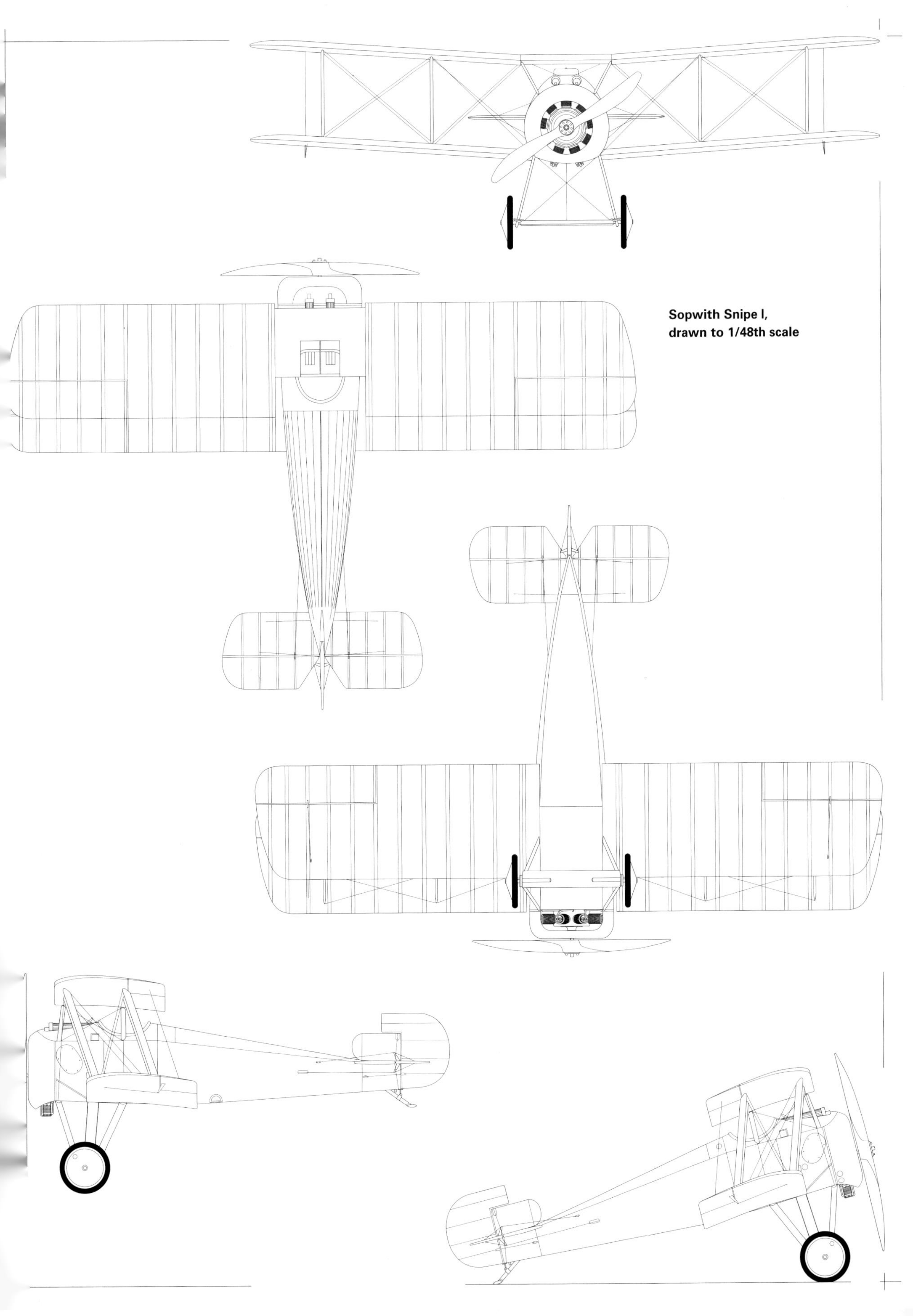
Sopwith Snipe I,
drawn to 1/48th scale

COLOUR PLATES

1

Dolphin C3829 of Capt J Leacroft, No 19 Sqn, Spring 1918

This machine served with No 19 Sqn from early 1918 until 7 October (a long period in frontline service for an aircraft in World War 1), at which time it was declared 'war weary', with the front part of the fuselage becoming saturated with oil. C3829 carried the squadron marking of a white dumbbell aft of the fuselage roundel, as well as the individual letter 'V' (although it is thought that at one point it also carried 'P'). The aircraft also had red wheel covers. Capt Leacroft's first claim (a Pfalz D III) in this machine came on 17 March 1918, and it was later flown by Capt F McQuiston DFC, who downed its last victim (a Fokker D VII) on 5 October. In all, C3829 accounted for 13 enemy machines, five being credited to Leacroft, two to J DePencier and six to McQuiston. When the fighter was retired, it had flown 242.5 hours.

2

Dolphin C3792 of Capt P Huskinson, No 19 Sqn, March 1918

Marked with the individual letter 'N', C3792 claimed its first victory with Capt Huskinson at the controls on 8 March 1918 – he would down his last four victories in this machine, bringing his score to 11. It was then taken over by Capt M R N Jennings in late March (one claim) and Capt R A Del'Haye in June (four claims), plus another whilst being flown by Lt C V Gardner (while coded A). C3792 was lost on 17 July when 2Lt R E White was shot down by Leutnant Otto Franke of *Jasta* 30 and taken prisoner. It had flown a total of 141 hours (see also profile 8).

3

Dolphin C4017 of Maj A D Carter, No 19 Sqn, Spring 1918

Marked with the letter 'I', C4017 first tasted success with Maj Carter on 15 March (his 16th victory), and by 8 May its pilots had claimed a further nine kills. 'Nick' Carter's next three victories were scored whilst flying C4132, but returning to C4017 on 19 May, he was shot down by Leutnant Paul Billik of *Jasta* 5 (he was the German's 16th victory) and taken prisoner.

4

Dolphin C3833 of Lt J A Aldridge, No 19 Sqn, Summer 1918

Lt Aldridge used C3833 to claim all five of his victories between April and September 1918. The Dolphin carried the individual letter 'J' behind the squadron's dumbbell marking. Flying more than 193 hours, this machine was finally taken off strength on 10 October after the front part of the fuselage had become saturated with oil – seemingly a common problem with war-weary Dolphins.

5

Dolphin C3796 of Lts A B Fairclough and A W Blake, No 19 Sqn, Summer 1918

C3796 did not enjoy a promising start to its operational career, for it was damaged in a collision on the ground at No 1 ASD on 15 February. Once repaired, however, it was issued to No 19 Sqn, and flown by aces Lts A B Fairclough and A W Blake, who scored four and two victories, respectively, with it. The fighter was marked with the individual letter 'S', and by the time it was sent away from No 19 Sqn for a major overhaul on 9 August 1918, it had flown over 136 hours.

6

Dolphin C4129 of Lt L H 'Hec' Ray, No 19 Sqn, Spring 1918

Lt Ray claimed three of his seven victories with this aircraft. A fourth kill for this machine came on 6 June 1918 when Lt C V Gardner (who would end the war with ten claims) scored his first victory. C4129 served with No 19 Sqn from 25 April through to 14 October. On this date it force landed at St Omer after being damaged by flak, and four days later it was struck off permanently as 'time expired'.

7

Dolphin C3799 of Capt G B Irving, No 19 Sqn, Summer 1918

Flown by Capt G B Irving DFC, this machine boasted a most unusual scheme inspired by its pilot. Aside from the normal camouflage, it had its entire engine cowling and forward upper plywood area aft of the cockpit painted blue. The tail fin and upper area of the tailplane were also finished in the same shade. Irving scored seven of his twelve victories in C3799, serving as a flight commander from May. The aircraft suffered damage on 1 August when Lt E S Ferrand ran into two other Dolphins whilst attempting to take off. It was duly sent to No 1 ASD for repair, by which time it had completed 169.5 flying hours.

8

Dolphin C3792 of Capt R A Del'Haye, No 19 Sqn, Summer 1918

Capt R A Del'Haye DFC scored his first five victories in C3792 during June-July 1918, before going on to D5236, in which he claimed his last four. This aircraft had previously been Pat Huskinson's 'N', but Del'Haye had the individual letter changed to 'A' aft of the dumbbell marking. C3792 had arrived on the squadron from No 1 ASD on 3 January 1918 (see also profile 2).

9

Dolphin C4019 of Capt J D DePencier, No 19 Sqn, Spring 1918

Wearing letter 'B', C4019 was used by Capt J D DePencier to score two of his eight victories. Their association lasted only a matter of weeks, however, for the machine was damaged on 21 May 1918 when its carburettor disintegrated and it was taken off squadron strength. C4019 had just 38.5 flying hours on its record log when it was dismantled and carted back to No 1 ASD, from whence it had come on 20 April.

10

Dolphin E4514 of Lt C M Moore, No 19 Sqn, Summer 1918

While not an ace, Lt Moore did score one of his four victories with this machine, and like C8087 (which had the word *INK* painted aft of its aircraft letter 'G') before it, E4515 featured the additional letters *LITE* painted inside the lower area of the 'E' to read *ELITE*. The fin of this machine was white, as were the wheel covers.

11

Dolphin C3899 of Lt N W Hustings, No 19 Sqn, August 1918

Adorned with individual letter 'D', C3899 served with the squadron until 1 September 1918, by which time it had been involved in eight successful combats. The fighter had been repaired following a mid-air collision on 30 June, and its engine seized over the unit's airfield at Cappelle on 1 September, resulting in the pilot having to perform a crash landing. It had flown more than 171 hours by the time it was written off.

12

Dolphin C4130 of Lt H N Compton, No 23 Sqn, October 1918

Lt Compton used C4130 to score his fourth and fifth victories in the last days of the war. Despite its early serial number, this machine did not appear on the squadron until October 1918. The fighter's individual letter was 'V', inside of which was added *IC* (in fawn paint) to form the word *VIC*. The 'V' was also repeated on the top fuselage decking. Also applied in fawn paint was a tiny lion on No 23 Sqn's white circle marking on the fuselage.

13

Dolphin C4150 of Lt H A F Goodison, No 23 Sqn, June 1918

Lt Goodison became an ace on Dolphins flying this machine in June 1918 when he claimed his fourth and fifth victories (having previously scored three flying SPADs). The fighter's 'Y' code was also repeated on the fop fuselage decking. C4150 served with No 23 Sqn from early 1918 (it was an ex-No 87 Sqn machine) until a loss of engine pressure on 29 June made it necessary for it to be struck off for major repair. C4150 had completed 79 flying hours by then.

14

Dolphin C3824 of Capt J W Pearson, No 23 Sqn, June 1918

Dolphin 'U' was used by American Capt J W Pearson DFC to gain the first three of eleven victories he scored with No 23 Sqn. The letter was repeated on the top fuselage decking and on the upper surface of the port wing, while the squadron's white circle unit marking was also repeated on top of the starboard wing. The fighter was damaged in a hard landing in mist and darkness on 1 July, Lt C E Walton having just claimed a victory with it during an evening combat. C3824 flew a total of 60 hours during five-and-a-half months of service with No 23 Sqn, arriving on the unit from No 1 ASD on 10 January 1918.

15

Dolphin E4717 of Capt H A White, No 23 Sqn, November 1918

Capt H A White DFC – another American serving with No 23 Sqn – flew E4717 as a flight commander late in the war. Although none of his seven confirmed victories were scored with this machine, it is believed that he claimed an unconfirmed success on 9 November. The Dolphin was sent to the unit from No 7 Aircraft Acceptance Park on 2 September, and White later described it as being 'the fastest machine on the squadron'. It was coded 'M', which was repeated on the upper port wing.

16

Dolphin D3669 of Capt A B Fairclough, No 23 Sqn, Summer 1918

Capt A B Fairclough MC flew D3669 with No 23 Sqn after having previously served with No 19 Sqn. He gained three of his twenty victories in this machine in June-July 1918, and also led a patrol which was credited with another kill. The aircraft had arrived on the squadron on 3 June, and was shot-up by a German fighter on 8 August whilst being flown by another pilot. Fairclough, as 'A Flight' commander, carried a white 'A' on the fuselage sides and top decking of his fighter. The Dolphin also boasted red wheel covers and a red rudder stabiliser.

17

Dolphin C3810 of Lt H N Compton, No 23 Sqn, July 1918

Although C3810 had the letter 'Z' painted on its fuselage, it does not appear to have had this repeated on the top wing. The fighter served with No 23 Sqn until 19 September, Compton claiming one confirmed kill with it on 7 July. It had completed 167.5 flying hours by the time it left the unit.

18

Dolphin C4131 of Maj N W Noel and Capts F I Lord and J D Canning, No 79 Sqn, Summer 1918

C4131 was flown by three pilots who achieved a total of six victories with it. No 79 Sqn CO, Maj N W Noel, scored one kill, American Capt F I Lord DFC claimed four, and the sixth victory was achieved by Capt J D Canning. It served with No 79 Sqn from 25 April through to 28 August, by which time it was deemed time expired and sent to No 1 ASD for a major overhaul. By then it had logged 211.5 hours. C4131 was unusual in that it had had its top plywood decking aft of the cockpit decorated with black and white squares. The individual letter 'T' was also repeated on both upper wing surfaces.

19

Dolphin D3727 of Lt E Taylor, No 79 Sqn, Summer 1918

American Lt E Taylor gained all five of his victories with D3727. Marked with the individual letter 'J' aft of the white squadron marking, which was repeated on the top port wing just inboard of the roundel, this aircraft served with No 79 Sqn from 16 June to 24 August, when it was lost in action. By then D3727 had completed 97 flying hours.

20

Dolphin C3879 of Capt R B Bannermann, No 79 Sqn, Summer 1918

Marked with the letter 'Q' aft of the squadron's white square, this machine arrived from No 1 ASD on 24 June 1918, and was on strength with the unit until 2 November. During this time it accumulated nearly 190 flying hours, and Kiwi ace Bannerman achieved 13 of his 17 kills with it. Note the fighter's all-white wheel covers.

21

Dolphin C3887 of Capt F W Gillet, No 79 Sqn, August 1918

Ranking Dolphin ace Capt F W Gillet DFC flew C3887, amongst others, during his long spell with No 79 Sqn. Despite this fighter completing 132 flying hours, recorded between its arrival from No 1 ASD and its return to the depot on 1 September 1918 due to an engine seizure, 'Razors' Gillet scored only his first three victories with the machine during August. Its individual aircraft letter was 'F' and, unusually, this was painted on the fuselage between the roundel and the white squadron square, rather than aft of the latter marking.

22

Dolphin E4589 of Capt F W Gillet and Capt L S Ladd, No 79 Sqn, Autumn 1918

American 'Razors' Gillet scored one of his twenty Dolphin victories in E4589 on 21 September, and this machine was later used by fellow flight commander Capt L S Ladd. The latter pilot claimed two victories with it on 14 October. E4589 carried the individual letter 'A', again before the square rather than after it, and the letter was repeated in white on the upper port wing just inboard of the roundel. E4589 was still serving with the squadron in Germany in 1919.

23

Dolphin H7244 of Capt F W Gillet, No 79 Sqn, Autumn 1918

Another of Capt F W Gillet's Dolphins was H7244. Note that its serial number appears in white on the fuselage rather than in the more standard white rectangular box. Its serial number reveals that it was a rebuilt machine, and the fighter wore the stylised letter 'S' aft of No 79 Sqn's white square marking. It was subsequently flown by Lt Henry with the occupation forces in Germany.

24

Dolphin D3584 of Capt F W Gillet, No 79 Sqn, Autumn 1918

Capt Gillet scored his final four victories in D3584, this aircraft being marked with the letter 'V' on the fuselage, aft of the white square. Photographs of this machine also show that it was periodically fitted with a bomb-rack for attacking targets on the ground.

25

Dolphin E4756 of Capt R B Bannerman, No 79 Sqn, November 1918

At war's end Capt R B Bannerman DFC was flying this machine, coded 'Q'. Note that its serial was painted in white on the fuselage (no rectangular box) and across the red, white and blue rudder marking.

26

Dolphin C8189 of Capt F J Stevenson, No 79 Sqn, Autumn 1918

C8189 was yet another No 79 Sqn Dolphin that featured a stylised letter – in this case an 'N'. The usual mount of Capt F J Stevenson DFC, the fighter was on squadron strength between 24 September and November 1918, having arrived straight from No 1 ASD. Stevenson succeeded in claiming three victories with it.

27

Dolphin C4159 of Lt A W Vigers, No 87 Sqn, April 1918

Lt A W Vigers MC DFC flew C4159 throughout his time in France, and the aircraft is depicted here as it appeared when he flew it to France in April 1918. The individual letter was 'C', repeated on the top starboard wing, and in France the 'lazy S' insignia was painted on the fuselage sides (see profile 32). When Vigers became 'B Flight' commander in August, the aircraft letter was changed to 'I'. Capt Vigers scored all 14 of his victories with this machine between 3 June and 23 September 1918, and a 15th was claimed by fellow No 87 Sqn ace Lt L N Hollinghurst on 4 October.

28

Dolphin C4168 of Maj J C Callaghan, CO of No 87 Sqn, Spring 1918

Maj J C Callaghan MC, CO of No 87 Sqn, flew C4168 to France in April 1918, where it was written off in a crash-landing on 20 May. It carried a white 'S' as its individual letter, and also featured a white shamrock insignia, denoting both its pilot's Irish ancestry and his former regiment in the Royal Munster Fusiliers. Callaghan later flew D3671, becoming an ace on 28 June, and it is likely that this aircraft carried the same markings as C4168. He was killed in action on 2 July, also flying D3671. The 'S' was repeated on the top upper starboard wing.

29

Dolphin C4056 of Lt C E Worthington, No 87 Sqn, April 1918

Lt C E Worthington usually flew aircraft 'L' during his time with No 87 Sqn, the future ace flying C4056 to France in April 1918. He later used it to score his first victory, and it was subsequently written off by another pilot on 18 July. Worthington then took over C4157, which had been Capt Pentland's machine, and he flew it regularly after the Australian ace was wounded on 25 August. He gained two victories with this aeroplane, which possibly retained Pentland's letter 'G'. 'Worthy' scored his fifth kill in D3590. Note the white centre circle on the wheel cover, denoting the aircraft's assignment to 'B Flight' (see also profile 35).

30

Dolphin C3827 of Capt A A N D Pentland, 'B Flight' commander No 87 Sqn, early Summer 1918

Capt A A N D Pentland MC DFC flew C3827 'G' during his spell as 'B Flight' commander. Jerry Pentland was already a SPAD ace with No 19 Sqn when he joined No 87 Sqn, and he claimed his 12th to 15th victories with this machine in the early summer of 1918. It was damaged in combat on 18 June when Pentland engaged two Rumpler two-seaters – the Dolphin had accumulated just under 39 flying hours by then. Note the flight commander's pennant affixed to the rudder. The letter 'G' was also repeated on the top starboard wing. Once the unit became established in France, its identity marking of a 'lazy' or 'horizontal S' was marked on the fuselage sides of its aircraft, aft of the individual letter.

31

Dolphin C4155 of Lt R M MacDonald, No 87 Sqn, May 1918

Lt R M MacDonald of No 87 Sqn flew C4155 to France in April 1918, and used it as his personal machine until he was brought down on 29 September and captured. The fighter's individual letter 'Q' was repeated on the top wing, and it was also marked with the 'lazy S' once in France. MacDonald achieved five victories with this Dolphin.

32

Dolphin C4159 of Lt A W Vigers, No 87 Sqn, August 1918
Marked 'I' from August 1918, Dolphin C4159 is seen here with its newly-applied squadron insignia and altered individual letter (see profile 27).

33

Dolphin C4136 of Lt L N Hollinghurst, No 87 Sqn, Autumn 1918
Lt L N Hollinghurst DFC of No 87 Sqn usually flew C4136 'J' (the letter being repeated on the top starboard wing). Of his 11 victories, plus a shared which he did not include, eight were scored in this machine. As with most 'B Flight' Dolphins, this aircraft features a white circle at the centre of its wheel covers.

34

Dolphin C8163 of Capt A J Larkin, 'A Flight' commander No 87 Sqn, Autumn 1918
Another high-scoring Dolphin in No 87 Sqn was C8163, flown by Capt A J Larkin DFC CdG, commander of 'A Flight'. Marked with fuselage letter 'A', repeated on the top starboard wing, it was his personal mount from August to December 1918, and he scored nine of his eleven victories in this aircraft. Larkin's first two claims were made flying C4173 (also marked 'A'), which was replaced by C8163 when it suffered carburettor trouble on 19 July after completing 57 flying hours. C8163 was eventually flown back to England on 19 January 1919. All 'A Flight' Dolphins had standard finish wheel covers.

35

Dolphin C4157 of Lt C E Worthington, No 87 Sqn, Autumn 1918
Lt C E Worthington's C4157, coded 'G', was formally the assigned aircraft of 23-kill ace Jerry Pentland. Worthington added the name *"Muddles"* beneath the Dolphin's cockpit rim. 'Worthy' scored two of his victories in this machine, making five in total for this No 87 Sqn Dolphin (see also profile 29).

36

Dolphin C4158 of Maj C J W Darwin, CO of No 87 Sqn, Autumn 1918
Maj C J W Darwin DSO took command of No 87 Sqn following the death of Maj J C Callaghan on 2 July 1918. Marked with the letter 'M' when he flew it to France in April, C4158 was later adorned with the 'lazy S', and remained on strength with the unit until 21 November. By then it had accumulated 152.5 flying hours, and apart from Johnny Darwin's five victories, Capt Pentland had scored a sixth in it on 14 August. It is not certain whether C4158 retained the 'M' after July, as this had denoted the 'C Flight' commander's aircraft, and it may have been changed – possibly to Callaghan's old 'S'.

37

Snipe E8013 of Capt G R Howsam, No 43 Sqn, Autumn 1918
E8013 was flown by Capt G R Howsam MC, and he used it to score his 13th, and final, victory of World War 1. Its squadron marking consisted of two white fuselage bars, one either side of the roundel, and these were followed by Howsam's personal letter 'F'.

38

Snipe E8069 of Capt T C R Baker, No 4 Sqn AFC, October 1918
Capt T C R Baker DFC MM served with No 4 Sqn AFC's 'B Flight', which meant that his aircraft featured an identifying number ('2'), rather than a letter, as was the case with the unit's remaining two flights. Tom Baker claimed his first Snipe victory (and his sixth kill overall) in this machine on 26 October 1918.

39

Snipe E8050 of Capt E R King, 'A Flight' commander No 4 Sqn AFC, Autumn 1918
Capt E R King DSO DFC flew this Snipe, marked with the letter 'A', whilst serving as 'A Flight' commander with No 4 Sqn AFC. He claimed his final seven victories of the war in E8050, which brought his overall tally to an impressive 26 kills, 19 of which had been achieved with the Sopwith Camel. No 4 Sqn AFC's unit marking consisted of one small vertical white bar forward of the fuselage roundel, and individual letters or numbers (depending on the flight) aft of the roundel. Note the two tiny white inverted bars just visible on the fighter's fin. These are also present on Capt Baker's machine.

40

Snipe E8102 of Maj W G Barker, attached to No 201 Sqn, October 1918
This is the famous Snipe flown by Maj W G Barker DSO MC during his attachment to No 201 Sqn in France. Surrounded by a number of Fokker D VIIs whilst patrolling the frontline on his own on 27 October 1918, he was brought down and severely wounded, but managed a reasonable crash-landing – the machine flipped over onto its back, partly crushing its tail. Barker's personal marking consisted of five thin white bands around the rear fuselage aft of the fuselage roundel, this decoration partially reflecting the markings he carried on the Camel that he flew in Italy. The latter machine boasted seven white and six black bands in roughly the same area. Another feature of his Italian Front Camel that was also present on this Snipe was a small, red, flat-metal devil thumbing his nose with both hands, which was affixed to the front of the starboard Vickers machine gun.

Back cover

Dolphin C3944 of Lt F I Lord, No 79 Sqn, April 1918
American ace Lt F I Lord started his war flying with No 79 Sqn in C3944. With the individual letter 'N' on the fuselage, repeated inboard on the top starboard wing and in black on the underside of the lower port wing, this aircraft also featured white wheel covers. By 2 May 1918 it had inexplicably been returned to the depot with just 27 flying hours appearing in its flight log.

INDEX

References to illustrations are shown in **bold**. Plates are shown with page (including Wing Top Views) and caption locators in brackets.